Covenantal Worship

Covenantal Worship

Reconsidering the Puritan Regulative Principle

R. J. GORE JR.

FOREWORD BY JOHN M. FRAME

P&R PUBLISHING

P.O. BOX 817 • PHILLIPSBURG • NEW JERSEY 08865-0817

Page design by Tobias Design
Typesetting by Michelle Feaster

Printed in the United States of America

Library of Congress Cataloging-in-Publication Data

Gore, R. J., 1955–
    Covenantal worship : reconsidering the Puritan regulative principle /
R. J. Gore, Jr.
       p. cm.
    Includes bibliographical references and index.
    ISBN 0-87552-562-8 (pbk.)
    1. Worship. I. Title.

BV10.3 .G67 2002
264'.051—dc21

                                   2002030343

To Joan,
my gift from God

CONTENTS

FOREWORD

When I heard, in the early 1990s, that R. J. Gore had written a dissertation at Westminster Theological Seminary opposing the regulative principle of worship, I had to see it for myself. To criticize the Puritan view of worship in that citadel of Presbyterian orthodoxy seemed a bold move, even perhaps a bit foolhardy. But Gore satisfied his examiners at Westminster, and he impressed me with the high quality of his research and thinking.

Research and thinking are not always balanced in our circles. I tend to regard the proponents of the Puritan regulative principle as stronger in the former than in the latter area. My own writings on worship have sometimes been criticized as having the reverse imbalance, and I won't contest that. But Gore has done a marvelous job, not only of mastering the historical sources, but also of analyzing them carefully and using that analysis to make balanced recommendations for our worship today.

I differ with him on a few points, mostly terminological. He defines "regulative principle" as including all the elements and distinctions made by the Puritans, and in that sense he rejects the regulative principle. I define it more generally as the principle that worship must be according to Scripture, and in that sense I affirm it. But as I read Gore, there is no substantive disagreement between us. We both want to say that Scripture must direct our worship, but that Scripture must be read according to sound hermeneutics. I am also less enthusiastic than Gore over the term *adiaphora*, for reasons similar to those of Shepherd, whom he cites, but I can affirm the points Gore makes when he uses the term.

If Christians (particularly Reformed ones, but others as well) consider this book thoughtfully and prayerfully, it can be a great help to us in ending the worship wars. Gore knows and deeply respects the thinking of Calvin, the Puritans, and the older Scots Presbyterians. But he also wants for us to observe the way God regulates worship in Scripture itself and to follow that biblical pattern, commanding what God commands, forbidding what God forbids, and leaving to the liberty of the church what God neither commands nor forbids. Both those who emphasize the need for a historically authentic Reformed worship and those who emphasize an authentically biblical worship applied to the present needs of the church can learn together from Gore. He expounds biblical criteria for worship that are common to all Reformed Christians and that can serve, therefore, as God-given means of uniting or reuniting us.

JOHN M. FRAME

ACKNOWLEDGMENTS

*T*he gestation process for this volume, a fairly significant revision of my dissertation at Westminster Theological Seminary (1988), has been long and difficult. My duties at Erskine Theological Seminary have occupied much of my time. My efforts to complete this work have taken me away from my family on many evenings and weekends. I want to express my appreciation to Joan, my wife, and to Matthew, Colin, and Alison, children of the covenant, for bearing with my many absences and ongoing preoccupation with "the book."

Over the years, key individuals have played an important part in the unfolding of the ideas contained in this book. During my years of doctoral studies, I was privileged to be pastor and friend to Mark and Ida Smith and Paul and Pat White. Their loving support and toleration of my thinking out loud was invaluable. In 1996, Randy Ruble, dean emeritus of Erskine Theological Seminary, hired me to come to Due West and teach systematic theology. Without this call, I probably would not have undertaken this project. Also, my thanks to John Carson, president of Erskine College and Erskine Theological Seminary, who has been a friend and encourager in my labors here at Erskine.

I also want to express my appreciation to my colleagues at Erskine Theological Seminary, beginning with my administrative assistant, Kathy Kay. She skillfully handles a multitude of responsibilities including many details that were necessary for this book to be completed. A special word of thanks goes to Don Fairbairn, Dale Johnson, Mary-Ruth Marshall, and Sherry Martin. Each one read the manuscript in its entirety and offered many helpful suggestions. My thanks also to Nathan Frazier, my graduate assistant, who helped me with many technical matters and was brave enough to offer several suggestions to improve the manuscript as well. I have benefited greatly from all their assistance. Any deficiencies in the ideas presented or the manner of presentation remain my own.

Finally, let me offer a word of appreciation to Clair Davis and Will Barker of Westminster Theological Seminary. Both served as advisors during my doctoral studies, and each, in his way, had a tremendous impact on my thinking. They taught me better than I learned (a fact I hope is not too painfully evident in the pages that follow). Anything good in this work can be attributed, in the first place, to the grace of God and, in the second place, to the influence of Westminster's godly faculty and these two men in particular.

ABBREVIATIONS

ICC	International Critical Commentary
ICR	John Calvin. *Institutes of the Christian Religion.* 1559 edition. Edited by John T. McNeill. Translated by Ford Lewis Battles. Library of Christian Classics 20–21. Philadelphia, 1960.
ICR 1536	John Calvin. *Institutes of the Christian Religion.* 1536 edition. Translated by Ford Lewis Battles. Grand Rapids, 1975.
ISBE	*International Standard Bible Encyclopedia.* Edited by G. W. Bromiley. 4 vols. Grand Rapids, 1979–88.
NICNT	New International Commentary on the New Testament
NIDNTT	*New International Dictionary of New Testament Theology.* Edited by C. Brown. 4 vols. Grand Rapids, 1975–85.
TDNT	*Theological Dictionary of the New Testament.* Edited by G. Kittel and G. Friedrich. Translated by G. W. Bromiley. 10 vols. Grand Rapids, 1964–76.
ZPEB	*Zondervan Pictorial Encyclopedia of the Bible.* Edited by M. C. Tenney. 5 vols. Grand Rapids, 1975.

INTRODUCTION: THE LONG AND WINDING ROAD

*T*oday, there is great confusion among evangelical Presbyterians over the theology and practice of worship. This is not meant to imply barrenness in practice, for indeed there is much diversity in the practice of worship throughout the Presbyterian churches. Rather, the confusion comes from the absence of a consensus, the lack of a coherent theology of worship that is based upon certain bedrock, widely accepted principles. As stated by Presbyterian minister Terry Johnson, "For the first time in 400 years, a consensus as to what constitutes Presbyterian worship is nowhere to be found."[1] While accurately reflecting the current state of affairs, Johnson's observation is somewhat overstated. In fact, this is not an entirely new situation. Consider, for example, the remarks made a century ago by the moderator of the General Assembly of the Presbyterian Church in the U.S.A. He lamented and criticized the "heterogeneous and irresponsible license which in our day has come to be known as Presbyterian worship, wherein every Presbyterian minister does that which is right in his own eyes."[2]

This book is the result of one Presbyterian minister's journey, a journey that involved my struggles with many issues of worship, particularly the principles involved in the regulation of worship. Furthermore, this journey involved my search for biblical stan-

1

dards for worship and the appropriate manner of expressing those standards in today's world. My undergraduate education and graduate theological education provided me with little background and preparation for these issues. At no point in my educational experience was I required to take a course in worship. Electives in worship were few and infrequently scheduled. Little was said officially about the importance of worship, and no explanation for the lack of academic emphasis was ever offered.

Nevertheless, I believe I understand the reason why no required courses in worship were included in any of the programs of study I pursued. Quite simply, the "powers-that-be" did not think that a very tight, full course of study should waste curriculum hours on a subject that we (faculty and students) already understood. That is to say, since we were all active in the church and attended worship regularly, we should know how to do worship! And knowing how "to do worship" is really all we should be concerned about anyway. Pastoral theology courses would touch on the hard stuff—weddings, funerals, and the sacraments—but there was no need to waste class time learning to do ordinary worship. Whether the academic community was predominantly fundamentalist, evangelical, or Reformed, all appeared to be in agreement on one thing at least: only liberals and "closet papists" were concerned with liturgy. Bible-believing folks, especially Reformed Christians, already knew how to worship.

The question of what constitutes proper worship did not concern me until I found myself installed as pastor of a church that had only recently been received into the presbytery. For years the church had been independent. The Sunday morning order of worship was striking in its lack of integrity. Numerous pastors had tinkered with it over the years, adding here, deleting there. The order of worship lacked any real sense of coherence. Serious revision was required.

I had been brought up as a teenager and young adult in fundamentalist Baptist circles. Only recently had I embraced the Reformed faith. Everything I knew about Presbyterian worship I had learned by attending Presbyterian churches over the previous four years. Nevertheless, I found it easy to give direction to the session. I knew how Presbyterian worship should be done! With confidence, I pulled out a copy of the old Book of Common Worship and my collection of Sunday bulletins from other evangelical Presbyterian churches. It took only a few minutes to identify the parts of worship common to them all—and cobble them together as *our* version of Presbyterian worship.

No doubt our order of worship looked very much like that in the majority of the churches in our presbytery. But not one elder in our session—pastor included—could give a thorough explanation for why we did what we did, why we left out certain expressions of worship, or why we placed the selected particulars in the prescribed order. The invocation and the benediction were easy enough. But it became progressively more difficult to explain our order of worship beyond that. What we did, we did in ignorance of any principle more profound than the conviction that we should be guided by Scripture and the Reformed tradition. The cash value of that understanding meant that we should do what other good Presbyterians were doing. Nevertheless, this early experience in worship renewal created in me a desire to understand more fully what we did in worship—and why.

My interest in matters of worship was piqued further by three important but unrelated factors. The first and most compelling factor was my ongoing academic career. As I began doctoral studies at Westminster Theological Seminary, I became fascinated with the simplicity of Puritan Reformed thinking. In particular, the Puritan regulative principle of worship seemed to cut the Gordian knot in matters of worship. Rather than endless discussions about right and wrong, Puritans simply banned everything that did not have explicit biblical warrant. Anything that was not commanded, or logically based on a command, Scripture did not allow. That certainly ended the guesswork.

Presbyterians are in large part modern heirs of the Puritans. The assembly at Westminster rejected the partial reformation embraced by Episcopalians and Lutherans. Quite simply, Presbyterians refused to tolerate the liturgical "rags of Rome"! Impressed with the consistency of Puritan thought, I desired to put the Puritan regulative principle of worship into action. In my local congregation, I sought to purge the sanctuary of the brass cross and the candlesticks on the communion table. Over the course of several weeks, first the candles and then the cross simply disappeared! Finally, the offering plates were banished from the communion table, and the table, at last, was restored to its one purpose—with purity. By the time anyone noticed what had happened, I had established a new tradition.

The last item to fall under the scrutiny of my developing Puritanism was the wooden cross behind the pulpit. As it turned out, a dearly beloved church member had given the cross to the church only a few years before. It replaced a rather unattractive portrait of Christ. I was ever so grateful that such an unmentionable affront to the second commandment was gone, but I was unsure how to remove the cross without creating controversy among the members of the church. Seeking guidance, I ran this issue by my doctoral advisor, Clair Davis. I hoped that his wisdom would point the way so that finally I could purge the building of this last vestige of "will-worship."[3] His response was the catalyst that forced me to begin rethinking what I thought was a matter fully settled. He said, "Before you take the cross down, ask yourself this question: What does it mean to the people—and what message will your moving it communicate?"

As I reflected on this challenge, it slowly dawned on me that to the church members, the wooden cross in the sanctuary was an important visible, physical, tangible symbol, not unlike the literary symbol of the cross that is used throughout Scripture. I knew the Puritan *applications* of the second commandment, but I could not shake the *implications* of the Bible's own use of the cross as metaphor, or literary symbol. For my church members, the wooden cross was simply the visible metaphor of all that they believed. It was the symbol of the crucified and resurrected Christ — the essence, the heart and soul of Christianity. Finding this issue not to be as black and white as I had originally assumed, I reserved final judgment for later. Could it be that a tangible figure was somehow sinful while a literary figure was quite acceptable? For the time being, I took no action and there was peace in the church. I did not have time to work through all the issues raised by this symbol. However, I was confident that once I finished my course work, I could devote the time required to resolve these issues conclusively.

The second factor that influenced my thinking came out of my experience in the life of the church. One winter I attended a stated presbytery meeting during which the host pastor presented an order of worship unlike anything I had ever seen in a Presbyterian church. I knew of the Nicene Creed, but had never used it in worship. I had never seen a congregation participate in a litany, and the notion of a written, corporate prayer was only a distant memory from my early Methodist childhood. Yet as the service of worship unfolded, I found myself uplifted by these expressions of worship. They enabled the members of the congregation to become participants, not merely spectators in worship. Furthermore, I noticed that no one in the presbytery was building a gallows to hang this pastor for his "un-Presbyterian" behavior. I was not sure of the full significance of what I had seen, but I longed to see that same spirit of participation in my congregation. Nevertheless, I still held to the Puritan regulative principle of worship, thinking that there must be some way to reconcile what I had experienced with what I professed to believe.

The third and final factor that shaped my thinking was, in God's providence, a career move with unexpected consequences. In July 1986, I was commissioned as a chaplain in the Army National Guard. As my doctoral studies drew to a close, I had begun to look about for other challenges and opportunities for ministry. Through a series of closed and opened doors, I found myself in January 1987 at the United States Army Chaplain Center and School, Fort Monmouth, New Jersey. My initial enthusiasm over becoming an Army chaplain was soon dampened. Within a few days of arriving, I discovered that I was expected to participate in what the Army called the collective or general Protestant service. These services, designed to accommodate Protestants of all stripes, did not look very Reformed. They even had a widely used, though not prescribed, altar setup. Indeed, I found myself once again facing a brass cross and candlesticks. Fortunately, Army regulations provided a loophole. I knew the regulations stipulated that I could avoid doing anything that violated my conscience, so long as I could demonstrate good reason why I was unable to participate.

This, I thought, could be done easily. I would look up all the books and articles on the Puritan regulative principle of worship and build my case. And so my search began. As I turned up books and articles, I found a very disturbing pattern. Many of the writings borrowed heavily from other sources favorable to the Puritan regulative principle of worship and provided little interaction with current developments in worship. There was much indicting of "will-worshipers," but little effort was made to articulate a positive exposition of the regulative principle in light of cultural challenges. Indeed, a great deal of the literature was little more than sloganeering. Furthermore, the exegesis of the key texts upon which the principle was based often appeared overstated and unconvincing.

The more I found the literature to be unsatisfactory, the more my interest grew. Before completing the officers basic course, I had determined to change my dissertation topic in order to complete a thorough study of this principle.[4] I believed that the Puritan regulative principle of worship provided the best expression of biblical truth, even if it had been misapplied or abused at one time or another. Surely, all it needed was some careful exegesis and sympathetic application to the issues that faced the church late in the twentieth century. Little did I know that my research would lead to conclusions that challenged much of what I had believed previously about Reformed worship.

There is one final thought that may help explain my journey. As I contemplated the research mission before me, I was sobered by the fact that so few Christians embraced the Puritan regulative principle of worship. For example, according to current statistics, there are 2,100,000,000 Christians in the world.[5] Presbyterians, in the United States, number 4,985,000 or about .24 percent of all those identified as Christians. Evangelical Presbyterians in the United States number about 400,000, or 8 percent of all Presbyterians in the United States or .019 percent of all Christians worldwide.[6] Of this number, an even smaller subset would profess to follow the Puritan regulative principle of worship. Even if one added to this sum the number from other bodies (Reformed Baptists, for example) who adhere to the Puritan regulative principle of worship and then expanded the number to include all estimated adherents worldwide, it is hard to imagine the number ever reaching statistical significance.

Now, the lack of adherents, in and of itself, does not negate the Puritan regulative principle of worship. But in light of the enormous witness against the principle, it is appropriate for Presbyterians to address the issue with a great deal of humility, asking if there is anything that we in the Presbyterian churches might learn from the church catholic.

To that end, I submit this work. What you read in these pages is the product of twenty years of research, reflection, worship, and dialog. I offer it not as the final word on the regulation of worship, but as a modest attempt to further the discussion. It is my prayer that this work will facilitate fruitful dialog within the Presbyterian churches and, to some degree, enable the church to find a more excellent way to glorify the great head of the church, who alone is worthy of our best efforts in worship.

Chapter 1

DOING YOUR OWN THING

*A*t the heart of a theology of worship is its foundational or formative principle(s) or, to use a good Presbyterian phrase, its "regulative principle." Historically, Presbyterians came to adopt a very strict principle governing worship, the Puritan regulative principle of worship. The Puritan regulative principle "teaches that with regard to worship whatever is commanded in Scripture is required, and that whatever is not commanded is forbidden."[1] That principle has been variously applied and increasingly ignored by contemporary Presbyterianism.[2] In fact, there are very few Presbyterian churches today that adhere to this principle strictly. Not only is the Puritan regulative principle of worship not widely followed, but also there is no other substitute principle that has received widespread acceptance among Presbyterians.

This does not mean that there are no other principles at work. At least five different approaches (based on as many different principles) can be identified in the Western church today. First, there is the "pragmatic" approach, which argues, in practice if not in

9

theory, that whatever works is allowed. This is often the theory underlying much of "free church" worship, particularly in the United
States. Second, there is the Roman Catholic "ecclesial" approach,
which maintains that whatever the church deems to be correct is
allowed. Third, there is the Lutheran (and Anglican) approach,
which contends that "whatever the Bible does not forbid is allowed." Fourth, there is the Reformed or Covenantal approach (as
advocated in this volume), which says, "Whatever is consistent
with covenant faithfulness is appropriate" in worship. Fifth, and finally, there is the Puritan approach, which contends, "whatever is
not commanded is forbidden." Strange as it may seem, it is possible to find examples of most of these approaches in modern Presbyterianism.

Even the most casual observer can see clearly that there is no
consensus on how to regulate Presbyterian worship. For example,
there are some situations in which apparently no formal principle
regulates the worship practices of a congregation. A congregation
may demonstrate the absence of any formal principle in at least
two ways: by the incoherence of the various parts of the service, or
by the apparent lack of direction in the order of worship. In such
instances there is an unhappy consistency that joins together an inadequate basis for worship with a flawed performance. Indeed, for
some Presbyterian congregations, little more than practical (pragmatic) considerations govern their activities in corporate worship.
For example, that which is artistically attractive or emotionally appealing may be brought into the order of worship with little concern for its biblical basis. Examples of such practices might
include the use of altar calls or some types of prerecorded or
canned special music.

Other situations exist in which a happy inconsistency is the
rule of the day. A defective or even absent foundation for biblical
worship is coupled with worship practices that show remarkable
conformity to biblical patterns. Here it is evident that the piety of
a congregation has inadvertently exceeded its theological insights

and understanding. One could argue that the historic principle, *lex orandi, lex credendi,* "the law of prayer is the law of belief," underlies this inconsistency.[3] This principle affirms that what exists on the popular level, as an expression of piety, often works its way into more formal statements of belief. An example of this might be found in congregations that embrace the use of "Scripture songs" on practical grounds alone. For some, it is enough that such songs communicate well with young people. The more profound argument that encourages the use of Scripture songs on biblical grounds is not thoroughly pondered.

The opposite situation may be found as well, where a thoughtless adherence to traditional forms, once meaningful but now hopelessly out of date, undermines the effectiveness or relevance of worship for the worshiping community. Here, there is a stated desire to be biblical and there may be a firm commitment to the principles regulating worship. Unfortunately, those principles are lived out in worship forms that are theologically sound but culturally irrelevant. An example of this might be found in congregations that persist in using Jacobean English in prayer and worship long after the use of "thee" and "thou" has been abandoned in everyday conversation. Many contemporary Christians would find the use of such language in worship to be confusing at the very least.

Finally, there are congregations that seek to maintain their theological integrity while exploring the possibilities of vibrant, creative worship.[4] They pursue this goal with intentional awareness of their surrounding culture. Here a genuine desire to understand the principles regulating biblical worship is coupled with an equally intense desire to make worship meaningful to the worshiper. This, in my estimation, is the best of all possible situations. Honesty demands the admission, however, that this is all too infrequently the case in evangelical Presbyterian congregations.[5] Indeed, one does not have to look far to find deficient worship practices. And herein lies the dilemma we now face: Is the Puritan regulative principle of worship *the* touchstone in matters of worship? If we do not follow the Puritan regulative principle of worship, are we left with "doing our own thing"? Is it possible that there is a more excellent way, or are these two alternatives the only choices available?

LATE-TWENTIETH-CENTURY TRENDS IN EVANGELICAL WORSHIP

Liturgical renewal in the evangelical community in general, and the Presbyterian community specifically, has complicated the problem of regulating worship. To understand how evangelical Presbyterians have been affected by modern developments in worship, it is necessary to consider their responses in light of the larger cultural and ecclesiastical settings. In the past, there has been a historic tension between advocates of High Church worship and devotees of Low Church worship. These same concerns have surfaced as contemporary efforts to revitalize worship have branched off into two distinctively different approaches.

By definition, evangelicals are theological conservatives. As such, they generally display a reluctance to consider novelties in matters of faith and practice. Nowhere has this reluctance been more evident than the evangelical response to the renewal of worship. While the Second Vatican Council wrested the Roman Catholic Church out of the sixteenth century and into the twentieth, evangelicals appeared by and large uninterested. While the mainline denominations avidly pursued the renewal of worship in the sixties, many evangelicals viewed their efforts as simply another example of liberal Christianity's preoccupation with the latest trends. In the last two decades, however, evangelicals have been forced to rethink their traditional views on worship. The challenge to traditional thinking has come not from mainline denominations or from the Roman Catholic Church, but rather (ironically) from among the most theologically conservative elements in the church. Among the earliest to sound the challenge was the late

Ray Stedman in his 1972 volume, *Body Life.*[6] In this volume, Stedman confronted the evangelical community with questions about the nature of biblical worship.

Returning to the Scriptures as his guide, Stedman found warrant for novel practices in worship: open requests for prayer, immediate and spontaneous responses to those requests, the sharing of testimonies regarding the Lord's working, the use of contemporary music as a vehicle of praise, and an emphasis on every member's gifting by the Spirit for service. Soon thereafter, Robert A. Morey wrote *Worship Is All of Life* in an attempt to further the renewal of worship by encouraging openness to congregational participation.[7] A key concept in Morey's understanding of worship was his contention that corporate worship is largely affected by private and family worship. Along with Stedman, he challenged the evangelical community to rethink the biblical and cultural relevance of traditional worship practices.

This innovative, engaging "Body Life" approach to worship achieved widespread acceptance within evangelical circles. In addition to Stedman's contribution, several other influences led to this renewal of worship, including Calvary Chapel, Maranatha Music, and the charismatic movement's embracing of praise songs and choruses.[8] Coupled with the widespread presence of Scripture songs, these innovations have flourished and matured. Today this new style of worship, best described as the "Praise and Worship" movement, has become commonplace. While groundbreaking at the time, these innovations have become the normal pattern for worship as many evangelicals drastically altered their worship in order to reflect what they perceived to be a more biblical pattern than the traditional, formal Sunday morning service of worship. Continued reflection, innovation, and experimentation have led to contemporary worship structures designed to maximize spontaneity and participation. The result often is worship that is mature, thoughtful, and culturally relevant.

Another challenge has come to the evangelical community

from a different direction. Robert Webber of Northern Baptist Theological Seminary, from a traditional fundamentalist background,
has been instrumental in awakening evangelicals to key issues they
have traditionally ignored. Webber has challenged the evangelical
community to reconsider the nature of worship and to explore the
breadth of Christian liturgy, particularly those worship traditions
historically viewed as High Church, such as the Anglican tradition:

> For me, Anglicanism preserves in its worship and sacra-
> ments the sense of mystery that rationalistic Christianity of
> either the liberal or evangelical sort seems to deny. I found
> myself longing for an experience of worship that went be-
> yond either emotionalism or intellectualism. I believe I've
> found that for myself in the Anglican tradition. I also felt a
> need for visible and tangible symbols that I could touch,
> feel, and experience with my senses. This need is met in
> the reality of Christ presented to me through the sacra-
> ments. These three needs—mystery, worship, and sacra-
> ments—are closely related.[9]

Further, in a later publication, Webber offered some positive examples of restructured worship that clearly evidence his reliance
on early church and Reformation (particularly Anglican) worship
sources.[10]

A similar challenge to evangelicals has come from the pen of
another author raised in traditional fundamentalist circles,
Thomas Howard. In his volume, *Evangelical Is Not Enough*,
Howard invited other evangelicals to join him on the Canterbury
Trail. "Enough people are following a similar route to warrant our
using the term 'a movement in the church.' No one, of course,
may seize on his own interests and shout, 'This is what God is doing!' Nonetheless, something is causing thousands of stoutly evangelical men and women to inquire into matters of the greatest
antiquity and gravity."[11]

Howard further challenged evangelicals to restore the Lord's Table to a place of importance, as "the center of the liturgy."[12] Through these writings, Webber and Howard addressed the evangelical community at large with questions—and proposed answers that demand a hearing. Webber has since continued to pour forth a stream of works on worship, culminating in the massive work, *The Complete Library of Christian Worship*, which he edited.[13]

THE DEVELOPING DIALOGUE

Additional volumes, less radical in their proposals, also made claims for consideration by evangelicals. In 1975, Anne Ortlund published *Up with Worship*, attempting to revitalize worship within existing worship structures by focusing on nonthreatening alternatives to received practices.[14]

In another direction, Robert G. Rayburn, a Presbyterian writing for the evangelical public at large, went on record for a more meaningful, formalized style of worship in his 1980 volume, *O Come, Let Us Worship*.[15] Perhaps one of the best volumes produced by the evangelical community is *The Worship of God*, by Ralph Martin.[16] Martin provided significant biblical and historical data on worship, as well as thoughtful pastoral insights into applying principles of worship. Significantly, he interacted with much of the contemporary literature on the renewal of worship. Other additions to the evangelical dialogue included *Real Worship* by Warren Wiersbe and *Worship: Rediscovering the Missing Jewel* by Ronald Allen and Gordon Borror. Both books sought to refocus corporate worship on its biblical foundations and provide guidance for worship in the church.[17]

The publishing of a new journal, *Worship Times*, by Maranatha Music, and the devoting of an entire issue of *Leadership* journal to then-current topics in worship indicated further interest among evangelicals.[18] While these volumes do not exhaust all that is available on worship, they do represent the major offerings that framed initial evangelical discussions on the renewal of worship.

PRESBYTERIAN STIRRINGS

Curiously, even as the evangelical community as a whole was challenged in terms of both a more spontaneous worship and a more liturgically patterned worship, so the Reformed and Presbyterian community was challenged by parallel developments. However, there was at least one major difference between the response of the evangelical community and that of the Reformed/Presbyterian community. That difference was due to the particular nature of Presbyterian worship, namely, its professed adherence to the Puritan regulative principle. That principle of worship is the operative guide in Presbyterian worship, stating that true worship consists only in that which is commanded in Scripture or that which is necessarily deduced from Scripture.

Thus, all challenges to the practice of worship by Presbyterians should take this principle into account. Yet, in spite of the official commitment to a governing or regulating principle of worship, much of Presbyterian worship today appears to be little more than a concerted determination to "do your own thing." In response to the inadequacy of the status quo, two very different and very exciting alternatives to traditional Presbyterian practice occurred in the attempt to reform Presbyterian worship.

Worship That Is Relevant

On the one hand, there was a widely influential movement, begun in the Orthodox Presbyterian Church in the 1980s and later transplanted to the Presbyterian Church in America, that emphasized concerns quite similar to those of the "Body Life" churches.

This movement was associated with the name of its leading proponent, Jack Miller,[19] and churches adhering to its principles were called "New Life" churches. This movement staked out a position to the left of traditional Presbyterian practice. With little hesitancy to break with tradition, the so-called New Life churches questioned the validity of a formal, liturgical format for worship.

In place of the usual elements of Sunday morning worship, this movement instituted greater lay participation through sharing prayer concerns and witnessing, introduced the practice of lifting hands in worship, encouraged the singing of contemporary Scripture songs along with traditional hymnody, and refocused the church's worship towards evangelism and discipleship.[20] These efforts were defended in terms of making expressions of worship culturally relevant. Further, these practices, virtually unknown before in Presbyterian worship, were considered to be consistent with the Puritan regulative principle of worship.[21]

Worship That Is Reverent

On the other hand, another movement, that of the Association of Reformed Churches of Tyler, Texas, staked out a position to the right of traditional Presbyterian practice. Led by James Jordan and Ray Sutton, the "Geneva group," so called because of the now-defunct Geneva Divinity School, raised eyebrows as they argued forcefully for apparently novel practices in Presbyterian worship. While also professing allegiance to the regulative principle of worship (properly construed, of course), the Geneva group reinstituted the use of formal liturgies, rehabilitated the chanting of Psalms, clothed their ministers in clerical garb, observed the liturgical year, and instituted paedo-communion.

The theology behind most of the Geneva Group's practice was explained in Jordan's volume *The Sociology of the Church*.[22] For this group, worship was defined in terms of reverence, form, participation, and ritual. As Jordan noted, "The priesthood of all believers means we need whole-personed participation in worship.

Worship is a dance. It is a command performance. It is not a spectator sport."[23]

These two movements clearly paralleled the developments in the evangelical community at large. Thus, there were impulses at work in Presbyterian circles that have run in opposite directions. While these tendencies provoked no special concern in broadly evangelical circles, they did create tension and provoke controversy in Presbyterian circles because each laid claim to representing the proper regulation of worship. When these two movements are added to traditional, formal Presbyterian worship, along with the plethora of other principles at work, the problem of finding a consensus for the regulation of worship is compounded even further.[24] These tendencies continue even to the present.

Thus, at least three significant, diverse patterns of worship are discernible, each claiming to represent the regulative principle of worship faithfully. It is just such confusion that warrants our closer inspection of the Puritan regulative principle of worship.[25]

QUESTIONS . . . AND LIMITATIONS

What is the regulative principle? Where did it arise? Why is it so important to Presbyterians? And what does it say in response to the current trends in liturgical renewal? These are the questions that must be answered. But before answering them, it is necessary to define the problem more precisely and limit the boundaries of this study. While it will be necessary to consider some of the historical material involved in the formation of the Puritan regulative principle of worship, this study is not intended to be an exhaustive treatment of the historical issues.

Therefore, this study will focus on the following items: the teaching of the Westminster Standards (chapter 2); the Westminster Directory and the middle way (chapter 3); Calvin's view of the regulation of worship (chapter 4); Calvin's application of the regulation of worship (chapter 5); biblical teaching and dominical practice (chapter 6); life, worship, and *adiaphora* (chapter 7); and, finally, the covenantal regulation of worship (chapter 8).

This study is not intended to be primarily an exercise in exegetical theology. Nonetheless, since a true theology of worship must depend upon the teaching of Scripture, certain key passages will be considered as the need arises to structure more accurately biblical teaching on the regulative principle. Similarly, though this is not intended to be primarily a study in historical theology, it would be impossible to lay before the reader the true state of the controversy without adequately citing key sources—within their historical context. To that end, a sizable number of primary and secondary sources in the areas of church history and theology will be referenced. Again, though this is a study of the regulation of worship, it is not primarily a work on worship or liturgics in general. Nevertheless, many key works in the theology of worship and the history of liturgics will be consulted in order to develop a framework for our discussion.

A final consideration is in order. There are two dangers that may arise in any attempt to evaluate the work of the past and point the direction for the future. The temptations toward either a radical discarding of the wisdom of the past or a reactionary embracing of tradition are ever present. However, neither extreme would be a correct response. Concerning the pursuit of new directions, we find no better warning than that issued by Paul Hoon in his classic, *The Integrity of Worship:* "I have to say that much liturgical reform seems misconceived to me because our reformers have brought more sensitivity to culture than theological discrimination. They have not reliably established their points of reference nor lived deeply enough with the church's liturgical mind to avoid repeating the mistakes of their ancestors."[26]

This warning cautions us against trendiness and the subordination of eternal truth to the seductive claims of a particular cultural context. At the same time, Hoon warns against the uncritical acceptance of all that has preceded. "Liturgical theology, especially, is always tempted to become 'fortress theology,' to fasten psychologically on God as the 'Great Conserver' and slip into equating what is true with what is unchanging."[27]

Thus, this study is not intended to be an endorsement of any principle of worship *a priori*. Rather, the goal is an open discussion of the biblical and theological basis for regulating worship. This will be accomplished by a critical evaluation of the strengths and weaknesses of the Puritan regulative principle of worship. My hope is that this analysis will point the way toward a greater coherence in Presbyterian worship, as well as greater freedom from strictures that may more accurately be viewed as culturally conditioned, and not as divinely commanded. We have examined the problem of regulating worship in light of recent developments. It is now time to consider the historical roots of the problem in order to reach a comprehensive definition of the Puritan regulative principle of worship.

Chapter 2

DÉJÀ VU ALL OVER AGAIN

We have seen that the issue of Presbyterian worship has become ever so complicated at the end of the twentieth and the beginning of the twenty-first centuries. But this is nothing new! If we go back to the sixteenth and seventeenth centuries, we find the same arguments and issues that disturb the peace of our twenty-first-century church. In the words of Yogi Berra, "It's déjà vu all over again." Indeed, the conflicts of today's church were already present and were already disturbing the church at the time of the Westminster Assembly.

Why has the issue of worship been such a continuing source of controversy throughout Presbyterian history—up to and including this very day? To answer this question with integrity, we need to explore the historical origins of the Puritan regulative principle. In so doing, we will be able to place the regulative principle in its proper historical context.

Such historical understanding is especially important in a time when ministers profess adherence to, or adamantly oppose, the regulative principle of worship—without adequately understanding what it teaches and requires. It is not unusual in presbyteries of evangelical churches to hear candidates profess full acceptance of the Westminster Confession of Faith—including the regulative principle of worship—without understanding fully what they are professing to believe!

The reason for this cognitive disconnection lies in a misunderstanding of the historic Puritan regulative principle of worship. As we shall see, the regulative principle of worship, as codified in the documents of the Westminster Assembly, is a Puritan formulation. It has a clear historical origin and definable contours. Today, when the term "regulative principle" comes from the lips of many Presbyterian ministers and students of theology, it is used to describe a host of different understandings of Presbyterian worship. However, there is only one confessional form of the regulative principle of worship: the Puritan formulation contained in the documents of the Westminster Assembly.[1] To profess adherence to the "regulative principle of worship" without recognizing its historical origin and its narrow strictures is to mangle words and to confuse even further an issue that is already fraught with misunderstanding and difficulty.

THE ROOTS OF PRESBYTERIAN WORSHIP

One of the reasons for the confusion that characterizes the worship of Presbyterians may be found in the historical origins of Presbyterianism. James F. White, a leading expert on worship, has provided an analysis of Protestant worship traditions that identifies the roots of Presbyterian worship.[2] He finds four Protestant worship traditions that date from the sixteenth century: (1) Lutheran, (2) Anglican, (3) Reformed, and (4) Anabaptist. He properly includes Presbyterianism within the Reformed tradition.

However, White places Puritan worship, a seventeenth-century development and major influence on Presbyterian faith and practice, midway between Reformed and Anabaptist traditions of worship. According to White's analysis, Presbyterians must trace their liturgical lineage back not only to the practices of Zwingli, Calvin, and Knox, but also to the practices of the English Puritans. These traditions, while not totally incompatible, are yet sufficiently different to provide a tension that has reappeared regularly within Presbyterian history. As the pendulum has swung from High Church to Low Church, Presbyterians have alternately embraced liturgical themes and worship practices that reflect either Reformed or Puritan roots and emphases.

While Anglicans and Puritans engaged in a century-long dispute over worship, the most important statement on Puritan worship came from the Westminster Assembly, a convocation of divines that met from July 1, 1643, until February 22, 1649. Like all other historical writings, the documents of the assembly were influenced by the historical and theological contexts in which they were produced. Indeed, the fact that the documents involved theological reflection as well as practical application made them all the more susceptible to the theological dynamics and polemics of the age. This may be explained more fully in terms of the larger context and the more immediate context.

The larger context was that the assembly's documents were produced in reaction against the Roman Catholic Church. That is, the ongoing Reformation in England and Scotland was an attempt to recapture the purity of the early church by removing the doctrinal and practical developments of the medieval Roman Catholic Church. This provided the background from which all liturgical progress was made. Thus, "the very questions they asked were determined by the times in which they asked them, as were the answers they received."[3]

In true pendulum-like fashion, the corrective efforts of the Westminster Assembly were at times excessive. James F. White observes that "when the Reformers did rebel against prevailing practice, justifiable anger at contemporary abuses often led to the elimination of things of genuine value that had become distorted in the course of time."[4] Certainly this intriguing perspective on the liturgical efforts of the Westminster Assembly raises many questions that need further consideration.

The concern with Roman Catholicism is easily demonstrated by the assembly's stated goals of achieving a religious consensus among the churches of Scotland, England, and Ireland. The Solemn League and Covenant of 1643 had expressed the legal basis of religious reform in the three kingdoms (England, Scotland, Wales) and gave direction to the Westminster Assembly. This document was predicated upon the conditions expressed in the prior Scottish National Covenant, which originally dated from 1581 and stated the case for national reform. It would be difficult to conceive of a document more polemically anti–Roman Catholic than the National Covenant.

In 1637, King Charles I had sought to impose an Episcopal structure and the Book of Common Prayer upon the Scottish church. The Scots viewed these developments as a step back toward Rome and opposed this imposition. Eventually, this controversy led to civil war. During the civil war, the English Parliament allied itself with the Scots, affirming the Solemn League and Covenant in 1643. This led to the Westminster Assembly, which sought to establish religious uniformity based on the Scottish (Presbyterian and Reformed) model. It would have been impossible to avoid entirely the strong anti-Catholic sentiments of the Scottish Covenanters.[5]

The more immediate context of the assembly concerns the status of the church in England. At this time the controversy between Anglicans and Puritans had reached a fever pitch. Nearly a century of controversy had made it clear that further attempts to correct the Book of Common Prayer were futile. The consensus was in favor of writing a new source book for worship. The final product represented the abandonment of the English liturgy and the conscious attempt to construct a new pattern of worship acceptable to the various parties present at the assembly, particularly the Scottish Presbyterians. In other words, the work of the assembly must be viewed as a reaction both to Roman Catholicism and to Anglicanism. This provides the necessary background for understanding many of the concerns expressed in the documents of the assembly.

The assembly's documents are the Westminster Standards (namely, the Westminster Confession of Faith, the Larger Catechism, and the Shorter Catechism).[6] The Larger Catechism expands on some points taught in the Westminster Confession of Faith and will be referenced when relevant to the doctrine of the confession. The Form of Presbyterial Church Government, although significant by virtue of the extended controversies that produced it, makes no direct contribution to the discussion at hand.[7] The Directory for the Publick Worship of God is also significant for this discussion. First, the Standards will be examined in order to establish the doctrinal formulation of the regulative principle. Then, the Westminster Directory will be examined in the next chapter to see the outworking of the Puritan principle in the practice of worship. Together, these documents will provide a complete definition of the Puritan regulative principle of worship.

THE CONFESSIONAL BASIS OF THE REGULATIVE PRINCIPLE

There are three important sections in the Westminster Confession of Faith that, when combined, present a coherent and comprehensive exposition of the Puritan regulative principle of worship. These sections include chapter 1 ("Of the Holy Scriptures"), section 6; chapter 20 ("Of Christian Liberty, and Liberty of Conscience"), section 2; and chapter 21 ("Of Religious Worship and the Sabbath Day"), sections 1–6. Each section will be examined in order to determine its distinctive contribution to a complete definition of the regulative principle.

The Larger Catechism has many helpful comments on various elements of worship in questions 156–96, including the reading and preaching of the Word, the proper observance of the sacraments, and the nature and practice of prayer. However, the questions most relevant to this discussion are questions 103–10 (on the first and second commandments). These will be referenced where appropriate.

Westminster Confession, 1.6

The first element of the regulative principle is established in the Westminster Confession of Faith, 1.6, where the following words are found:

> The whole counsel of God concerning all things necessary for His own glory, man's salvation, faith, and life, is either expressly set down in Scripture, or by good and necessary consequence may be deduced from Scripture: unto which nothing at any time is to be added, whether by new revelations of the Spirit, or traditions of men. Nevertheless we acknowledge the inward illumination of the Spirit of God to be necessary for the saving understanding of such things as are revealed in the Word: and that there are some circumstances concerning the worship of God, and government of the Church, common to human actions and societies, which are to be ordered by the light of nature and Christian prudence, according to the general rules of the Word, which are always to be observed.[8]

There are two main points established here that are relevant to this inquiry. First, all worship is either based directly on Scripture or is logically deducible from Scripture. Second, there are circumstances common to any human society that are not subject to explicit commands, but rather to general conformity to the Word and reasonableness.

Concerning this first point, which John Murray has described as "one of the most eloquent statements of the Confession," it is clear that the intent is to ground faith and practice in the Scriptures alone.[9] This is an obvious application of the Protestant concept of *sola scriptura*. Faith and practice are anchored to the Scriptures because the Scriptures reveal all that we need to know in order to live in covenant faithfulness. "The inspired Scriptures of the Old and New Testaments are a *complete* rule of faith and practice: they embrace the whole of whatever supernatural revelation God now makes to men, and are abundantly sufficient for all the practical necessities of men or communities."[10] This does not mean that every possible contingency in human life is considered in particular. Rather, the confession here makes it clear that biblical principles are so extensive in their scope that every possible contingency can be addressed by way of application.[11]

In reference to worship, it is the confession's intent to deny "will-worship" and to bind all legitimate worship to the express command of God. James Bannerman discusses this very point in his exposition on rites and ceremonies:

> The doctrine of the Westminster Standards and of our Church is, that whatsoever is not expressly appointed in the Word, or appointed by necessary inference from the Word, it is not lawful for the Church in the exercise of its own authority to enjoin; the restriction upon that authority being, that it shall announce and enforce nothing in the public worship of God, except what God himself has in explicit terms or by implication instituted.[12]

This section is the embodiment of Puritan thought on the regulative principle. The Puritan position is clearest when contrasted with the Anglican (or Lutheran) principle of worship, namely, "whatever is not forbidden, is allowed."[13] Note, for example, the difference in tone and spirit conveyed in article 20, "Of the aucthoritie of the Church," in the Thirty-Nine Articles, the confession of the Church of England:

> The Church hath power to decree Rites or Ceremonies, and aucthoritie in controuersies of fayth: And yet it is not lawfull for the Church to ordayne any thyng that is contrarie to Gods worde written, neyther may it so expounde one place of scripture, that it be repugnaunt to another. Wherefore, although the Churche be a witnesse and a keper of holy writ: yet, as it ought not to decree any thing agaynst the same, so besides the same, ought it not to enforce any thing to be beleued for necessitie of saluation.[14]

In Puritan thinking, the Anglican (or Lutheran position) was an abomination because it gave the church a prerogative that the Puritans believed belonged to God alone, namely, the right to regulate worship. George Gillespie, one of the Scots commissioners to the Westminster Assembly and a key figure in developing the Westminster position on worship, condemned the Anglican theory: "All sacred significant ceremonies of man's devising we condemn as an addition to the word of God, which is forbidden no less than diminution from it."[15] Similarly, Samuel Rutherford, another influential Scots commissioner, complained about the king's practice of prescribing worship not commanded in Scripture. All legitimate worship, he said, is "either expressly grounded upon the word of God, or by necessary consequence drawn from it, and so no commandment of men, but of God."[16]

John Owen, a proponent of the Puritan view (though not a commissioner at Westminster), wrote against the 1662 Act of Uniformity (which imposed the use of the Book of Common Prayer throughout all of England), brilliantly summarizing the Puritan position:

> But whereas God himself having instituted his own worship and all the concernments of it, doth also assert his own au-

thority and will as the sole cause and rule of all the worship that he will accept, no instance being left on record of any one that ever made any additions to what he had appointed, on any pretence whatever, or by virtue of any authority whatever, that was accepted with him; and whereas the most eminent of those who have assumed that power to themselves, as also of the judgment of the reasons necessary for the exerting of it, as to matter and manner, have been given up, in the righteous judgment of God, to do things not convenient, yea, abominable unto him (as in the papal church),—it is not unlikely to be the wisdom of men to be very cautious of intruding themselves into this thankless office.[17]

Here Owen gives expression to a key emphasis in the Westminster doctrine, for one of the sins noted in question 109 of the Larger Catechism involves the approval or use of "any religious worship not instituted by God Himself."[18]

However, in moving to the second point, it immediately becomes clear that a significant problem exists. The second point appeals to the general teaching of the Word and speaks of "some circumstances" that may be determined not according to explicit command but, rather, according to the more ambiguous concepts of universality, reasonableness, and prudence. In other words, there are two criteria that must be met to determine legitimate circumstances. First, whatever choice in circumstances one makes, it must be conformable to the Scriptures in general, "the general rules of the Word." Thus, whatever is done must be in accordance with the indirect, general teaching of Scripture where there is no direct, specific requirement applicable.[19]

Second, legitimate options within the category of "circumstances" must also be in accord with social decorum and custom. Both requirements are necessary, thus providing for a certain amount of adaptability as social customs vary depending upon time and place. The Puritan regulative principle of worship, then, will not necessarily result in a flat, uniform worship. There will, however, be extensive agreement in that the substantial, essential, or significant parts of worship (that is, those elements required by divine command or logical necessity) are identified in Scripture and are not subject to development through time or change across diverse cultures.

However, there is still a problem. To be specific, where (and how) does one draw the line between that which is circumstantial to worship and that which is an element of worship? A. A. Hodge attempted to resolve the question by speaking of this second point as having reference to "detailed adjustments to changing circumstances."[20] More recently, G. I. Williamson gave as examples of these circumstances "such things as the place and time (on Sunday) of congregational assembly."[21] Clearly the allowance for circumstances was not created to smuggle in through the backdoor substantial parts of worship, elements, under the guise of expediency or circumstances.[22] Yet, how does one identify these "detailed adjustments"?

Unfortunately, Presbyterian churches have never reached a workable consensus, much less a complete agreement on the identification or content of these circumstances. Edmund P. Clowney, a former professor of practical theology, gives a clear example of the difficulty presented by the distinction between elements and circumstances in his suggestion that the musical accompaniment of group singing is circumstantial.[23] By way of contrast, in the previous century, John L. Girardeau, a Southern Presbyterian theologian, presented the historic Presbyterian view, arguing that instrumental music would constitute an element of worship, that it is *not* commanded, and that instrumental music most certainly is *not* a mere circumstance to be determined by social custom or cultural concerns.[24] The difficulty in determining the respective boundaries of circumstances and of that which is regulated (elements) has been very clearly documented in the American Presbyterian church during the nineteenth and twentieth centuries.[25]

Perhaps a better way of distinguishing between what is commanded and what is circumstantial is to differentiate between what is essential and what is nonessential in worship. The essential is only that which has been divinely commanded in specific rules of worship. The nonessential, or circumstantial, has to do with other matters that answer to general rules of Scripture and human society. George Gillespie provided an extensive discussion of the nature of circumstances.[26] He said that three conditions must be met in order for anything to be a circumstance of worship and thus subject to the wisdom and discretion of the church.

First, a circumstance of worship is "no substantial part of it; no sacred and significant ceremony."[27] A circumstance of worship, then, would be something connected to a sacred act, but not an essential part of it, *circa sacra* not *in sacris*.[28] Second, circumstances are matters that are "not determinable by Scripture."[29] By definition, then, anything that is determined by Scripture is essential or substantial and therefore not subject to determination by the church. Third, circumstances subject to the will of the church are those for which "an evident reason exists" for their use.[30]

While this sounds somewhat ambiguous, Gillespie makes a key point. He says that even in matters that are not specifically addressed by divine command, there is nevertheless the requirement that sufficient grounds exist for their use. In other words, the church arranges circumstances (nonessentials) where necessary to the observance of the "elements" (essentials), but does not engage, on its own authority, with the multiplication and expansion of circumstances. "Even in the instance of arranging circumstances, there must be a sufficient reason, either in the necessity of the act, or in the manifest Christian expediency of it, to justify the Church in adding to her canons of order, and limiting by these the Christian liberty of her members."[31] To illustrate, it would be legitimate to determine that public prayer will occur on a given date, at a set time; it would be unlawful and a transgression of the Puritan regulative principle to require that one praying should bow to the east, or should prostrate himself before a religious statue.[32]

Thus, the first part of the definition of the Puritan regulative principle is that whatever has "a positive warrant" in Scripture for its use is instituted by God and justified for employment in worship.[33] The circumstances of its performance may be determined according to the principles found in all human society: common practice, reasonableness, and prudence. In spite of the efforts of the divines to clarify and specify the boundaries of biblical worship, there remain two basic ambiguities. First, there are still some difficulties in distinguishing essential worship from mere circumstance. Second, there is some confusion concerning the nature of the "positive warrant" from Scripture. Does this require an explicit command, or logical necessity based on explicit commands? Or is something less specific acceptable? For example, is it permissible to use doctrinally sound, uninspired hymns in worship? Does this practice have "positive warrant"?

These difficulties do not vitiate the Puritan regulative principle in and of themselves; they do, however, point out problems in its structure that may well indicate the need for further reflection and possible reformulation.

Westminster Confession, 20.2

The second element of the Puritan regulative principle is found in the Westminster Confession of Faith, 20.2, in the following words:

> God alone is Lord of the conscience, and hath left it free from the doctrines and commandments of men, which are in anything contrary to His Word; or beside it, if matters of faith or worship. So that, to believe such doctrines, or to obey such commands, out of conscience, is to betray true liberty of conscience: and the requiring of an implicit faith, and an absolute and blind obedience is to destroy liberty of conscience, and reason also.

The import of this passage is its strong denial of the right of coercion by civil or religious authorities. The specific application to the regulative principle includes several items.

First, God alone "has authoritatively addressed the human conscience only in his law, the only perfect revelation of which in this world is the inspired Scriptures."[34] The argument is that neither church nor state has the right to bind the conscience where there is no clear divine command. The response to question 105 of the Larger Catechism notes that one of the sins against the first commandment is "making men the lords of our faith and conscience."

Second, there are two kinds of rules that no authority has the right to legislate: (1) rules contrary to Scripture (in any area), and (2) rules in addition to Scripture (in matters of faith and worship). Rules contrary to Scripture would involve injunctions that would forbid the use of something not sinful in itself. G. I. Williamson gives as examples of rules contrary to Scripture "prohibitions requiring total abstinence from the use of certain material things."[35] Rules in addition to Scripture would involve requiring the performance of some task, duty, or act, or the belief in some doctrine not specifically required in Scripture. For example, it would be improper for the church to require that Christians believe in the immaculate conception of Mary. A. A. Hodge says, "Hence to believe such doctrines, or to obey such commandments as a matter of conscience, is to be guilty of the sin of betraying the liberty of conscience and its loyalty to its only Lord; and to require such an obedience of others is to be guilty of the sin of usurping the prerogative of God and attempting to destroy the most precious liberties of men."[36]

A further clarification of this section is in order. As previously noted, there are two distinct levels in regards to freedom of conscience. On the first level, the conscience is free from the church or state coercing or imposing *anything* that is contrary to the commands of Scripture. On the second level, the confession provides a more pointed guarantee of freedom concerning *anything that touches on matters of faith* (what one believes) *or worship* (how one expresses that belief). This applies not only where Scripture is clearly violated, but even where the thing commanded is simply "beside it," or not explicitly warranted. This most certainly addresses the issue of *adiaphora* and warns against binding the conscience, forcing it to believe or to observe that which is "indifferent."[37]

Therefore, in matters of faith and worship, the conscience of the believer is free from any practice that is not explicitly required by the Scriptures. As S. W. Carruthers explains, "The divines' argument is this: men are free in all things not directly contrary to God's word; but in addition, they are free in matters not stated in the word."[38] Thus, for the church to invent and impose additional requirements—not contrary to Scripture, but not commanded by Scripture, either—would be a violation of this principle.

Carruthers also notes that the usual reading of this passage is a weaker affirmation of this principle. Many editions change the semicolon after "Word" to a comma, and change "if matters" to "in matters." The Carruthers text, which has been cited above, rejects this reading in favor of a reading that provides even stronger guard against compulsion in *adiaphora*, or "matters indifferent." As the Carruthers text reads, "God alone is Lord of the conscience, and hath left it free from the doctrines and commandments of men, which are in anything contrary to His Word; *or beside it, if matters of faith or worship.*"

It must be noted that this section does not undermine the authority of the church or the state. It does, however, limit their respective power to what accords with God's authority. A twentieth-century Presbyterian theologian, George Hendry, provides additional insight into the confession's concern with the legitimate use of church authority:

> The Confession proposes two tests to determine whether the authority of the church is being used in that way or not.

The first is conformity to the word of God. Nothing that is contrary to the word, or "beside" it (i.e., not found in it, like certain orders of ministry or forms of church organization, which, though they may be sanctioned by ancient usage, are without express warrant in the word), can be held to be essential. The other test is liberty of conscience (in the more restricted sense of the phrase). If the church demands blind and unquestioning faith and obedience, that is inconsistent with the authority of God, which can be acknowledged only in freedom.[39]

Simply put, the second part of our definition states that only those things which are clearly required by the Scriptures, and therefore by God as the highest authority, can be required by any subordinate authority. The church, then, does not have the authority to impose anything in worship that is not required by the Scriptures. The Westminster Confession of Faith clearly teaches that the church does not have the authority to impose innovations in worship.[40]

Westminster Confession, 21.1-6

The third element of the Puritan regulative principle of worship is detailed in the Westminster Confession of Faith, 21.1–6. In this passage, a general reference to the regulative principle of worship is found in section 1. Specific applications of this general reference are then expressed in sections 2–6. Note the wording of section 1:

The light of nature showeth that there is a God, who hath lordship and sovereignty over all, is good, and doeth good unto all, and is therefore to be feared, loved, praised, called upon, trusted in, and served, with all the heart, and with all the soul, and with all the might. But the acceptable way of worshipping the true God is instituted by Himself, and so limited by His own revealed will, that He may not be worshipped according to the imaginations and devices of men, or the suggestions of Satan, under any visible representation, or any other way not prescribed in the Holy Scripture.

Although there are several subsidiary ideas in this paragraph, the key idea is the regulation of worship described in terms of a positive injunction and a negative prohibition. The positive injunction is very simple: acceptable worship is that which is instituted by God in accordance with his own will. In essence, this is but a reiteration of the first element in the Puritan regulative principle as seen in the Westminster Confession of Faith, 1.6. To the Puritan, this is the heart of the regulative principle, for to worship God in any way other than according to his commands is to commit the sin of idolatry.[41]

A. A. Hodge admits, in reference to this principle, that it may be argued that man in innocence could have worshiped God correctly without strict, positive commands. But he goes on to say that "since man's moral nature is depraved, and his religious instincts perverted, and his relations to God reversed by sin, it is self-evident that an explicit, positive revelation is necessary, not only to tell man that God will admit his worship at all, but also to prescribe the principles upon which, and the methods in which, that worship and service may be rendered."[42] As examples of the violation of this injunction, Williamson cites the offering of Cain, and the strange fire of Nadab and Abihu. They did not explicitly follow God's sanctions. "That which is instituted (commanded) by God is true worship. That which is not instituted by God is *for that reason* itself false worship."[43]

The negative prohibition clearly denies the legitimacy of any will-worship, that is, "anything and everything that men may presume to invent or to devise without such divine commandment."[44] This has to be interpreted in conjunction with "some circumstances" mentioned earlier in the Westminster Confession of Faith, 1.6. The difficulties here have been addressed in terms of the distinction between what is a substantial part of worship and what is merely accidental. Bannerman further clarifies this distinction.

> On the one side of the line that separates these two provinces, are what belong to Church worship so called,— the positive rites and ceremonies and institutions that enter as essential elements into it; and here the Church is merely Christ's servant to administer and to carry them into effect. On the other side of that line are what belong to the circumstances of worship as necessary to its decent and orderly administration,—circumstances not peculiar to the solemnities of the Church, nor laid down in detail by Christ, but common to them with other civil solemnities, and left to be regulated by the dictates of reason and nature; and here the Church is the minister of nature and reason, and her actions must be determined by their declarations.[45]

The confession is careful not to leave too much to the imagination, for it then proceeds in sections 2–6 to list the elements that constitute legitimate worship according to the positive and negative principles in section 1. These divinely prescribed elements are: (1) prayer, with thanksgiving (21.3–4); (2) the reading of Scripture (21.5); (3) preaching (and hearing) the Word (21.5); (4) singing of Psalms (21.5); (5) sacraments (21.5); (6) oaths, vows, fastings, and thanksgivings (21.5); and (7) keeping of the Sabbath (21.7–8). Compare this with the list of ordinances contained within the 1645 Form of Presbyterial Church Government: "The ordinances in a single congregation are, prayer, thanksgiving, and singing of Psalms, the word read, (although there follows no immediate explication of what is read,) the word expounded and applied, catechising, the sacraments administered, collection made for the poor, dismissing the people with a blessing."[46]

One writer has summarized the significance of the Westminster Assembly's views on worship: "As the sovereignty of God was the formative principle in their theology, so the sovereignty of God, the Son, was the shaping principle in their system of government and worship. The key in each case was the same. When they passed from doctrine to polity, or from polity to doctrine, or from both to worship, there was no break in the harmony."[47] Thus, the Puritan regulative principle of worship is quite simply the doctrine that only what God has instituted or commanded (or that which is a necessary, logical consequence of what God has instituted or commanded) may be an acceptable element of worship. Beside this there are circumstances of worship, no substantial or necessary part of worship, which are negotiable and variable depending on the particulars of a given situation.

This definition, which was codified by the Westminster Confession of Faith, was not an esoteric formulation, but rather it was common property of Puritans in general before the assembly, and later of all who received the documents of the assembly or adapted them for their own purposes as in the Savoy Declaration.[48] In other words, the basic tenets of the regulative principle of worship antedated the Westminster Assembly; the assembly's contribution was to raise the Puritan principle to confessional level.

As the influence of the assembly spread, the Puritan regulative principle, as officially expressed in the Westminster Confession of Faith and the Directory, became the basis of accepted Presbyterian worship. Even though the concept is quite old, the precise origin of the term "regulative principle of worship" is not known. While there are references to "regulating" worship, I have found no explicit references to the regulative principle of worship until the twentieth century.[49] In fact, in two turn-of-the-century works that make reference to the Covenanters, for whom the Puritan regulative principle of worship was (and continues to be) a distinguishing badge, no reference to this phrase is found.[50]

Now the fact that the Puritan regulative principle of worship was common property of all Presbyterians historically may be established by briefly noting comments by several influential theologians. Samuel Miller (1769–1850), noted professor of Princeton Theological Seminary, argued that worship must be scriptural. Miller objected to all elements in worship that were of human origin, utilizing the line of argumentation he found in Puritan sources.[51] For Miller, eighteenth-century Presbyterian worship was "the same mode of worship which we believe existed in the apostolic age."[52] He goes on to state the regulative principle in these words: "Christ is the only King and Head of the Church. His word is the law of his house. Of course the Church ought not to consider herself as possessing any power which that word does not warrant. If therefore, she cannot find in Scripture, authority, either direct, or fairly implied, to the amount contended for, she does not possess that authority."[53]

James Bannerman (1807–68), a Scottish theologian who has also had a significant impact on American Presbyterianism, succinctly defined the Puritan regulative principle in these words:

> The doctrine of the Westminster standards and of our Church is, that whatsoever is not expressly appointed in the Word, or appointed by necessary inference from the Word, it is not lawful for the Church in the exercise of its own authority to enjoin; the restriction upon that authority being, that it shall announce and enforce nothing in the public worship of God, except what God Himself has in explicit terms or by implication instituted.[54]

William Cunningham (1805–61), another Scotsman, also clearly articulated the Puritan regulative principle of worship. "The Calvinistic section of the Reformers, following their great master, adopted a stricter rule, and were of [the] opinion, that there are sufficiently plain indications in Scripture itself, that it was Christ's mind and will, that nothing should be introduced into the government and worship of the church, unless a positive warrant for it could be found in Scripture."[55] He goes on to note that this was the position of both English Puritans and Scottish Presbyterians, "the only true and safe principle applicable to this matter."[56]

Likewise, Robert L. Dabney (1820–98), a noted Southern Presbyterian theologian, in a discussion on the propriety of Sabbath worship, appeals to the received basis of worship to prove the legitimacy of Sabbath worship.

> If the great duty of worship is essentially and morally binding, this necessary provision for compliance is also essentially and morally binding. Whose is the reasonable and natural authority for providing and enforcing it? — the creature's or the Lord's? To ask this question is to answer it. Obviously, this provision ought to be fixed by the Lord, to whom the worship is due. It is his right to settle it. He alone has the authority to enforce it.[57]

Similarly, in discussing the import of the second commandment, Dabney prefaces his exposition with these words: "It may be said in general, that this commandment requires those acts and modes of worship for the true God which He hath required of us in His word, and prohibits all others. What Protestants call will-worship is forbidden."[58]

These few brief quotations indicate that the Puritan regulative principle of worship has had a significant place in Presbyterian history. Each of these men speaks of the principle as an integral part of his ecclesiastical identity. It is well defined, understood, and prominent in both American and Scottish Presbyterianism. However, further information is necessary to complete the picture. Therefore, we now turn to the Directory on worship.

Chapter 3

THE PURITAN VIA MEDIA

he Directory for the Publick Worship of God was completed by the Westminster Assembly at the end of 1644 and published by the authority of Parliament in 1645.[1] Approximately seventy sessions were spent in considering and altering the exact formulations of the document.[2] The committee given charge of producing the Directory consisted of four Scottish divines (Baillie, Gillespie, Henderson, and Rutherford), four English Puritans (Palmer, Goodwin—the only Independent, Herle, Young), and, as chairman, Stephen Marshall. The document consists of a preface, which explains the contemporary situation in England and establishes the need for the Directory, and further pericopes that address the particular parts of worship: (1) the assembling and behavior of the congregation, (2) the public reading of the Bible, (3) public prayer before the sermon, (4) preaching, (5) prayer following the sermon, (6) the administration of the sacraments, (7) observing the Sabbath, (8) the marriage ceremony, (9) visitation of the sick, (10) burial of the dead, (11) fasting, (12) days of thanksgiving, (13) the singing of Psalms, and an appendix dealing with festival days and places of worship.

It would be interesting to evaluate each pericope, but such would be beyond the scope of this work. Rather, the concern here is with the underlying basis of worship, the Puritan regulative principle of worship. Specifics will be cited only as they are necessary to illustrate this principle.[3]

CONTINUITY WITH THE WESTMINSTER STANDARDS

Although the Directory may properly be described as a compromise document, this description is primarily in terms of what is not required or not forbidden, rather than in terms of what is explicitly required or forbidden. The discussion in the Directory of what is clearly required is nothing other than a consistent insistence on the divine prerogative in worship. That is, even as the Westminster Standards later would define acceptable worship in terms of what God has commanded, even so the Directory is in agreement with that definition in its positive teachings. In terms of chronology, the Directory was completed before the Westminster Confession of Faith (which was completed April 29, 1647) and the Larger Catechism (October 15, 1647).[4]

However, as the evidence will indicate, the Directory at times chose to remain silent over certain issues that were sensitive to the various parties in order to achieve a broader acceptance. This is clearly articulated in the preface. In providing justification for undertaking the Directory, the assembly begins by describing the unhappy circumstances that prevailed under the reign of the Book of Common Prayer:

> For, not to speak of urging the reading of all the prayers, which very greatly increased the burden of it, the many unprofitable and burdensome ceremonies contained in it have occasioned much mischief, as well by disquieting the consciences of many godly ministers and people, who

could not yield unto them, as by depriving them of the ordinances of God, which they might not enjoy without conforming or subscribing to those ceremonies.[5]

The distaste for the Anglican liturgy was not a directionless reaction, but instead was part of a considered theology of worship
that had as its most basic thought the divine prerogative in worship.
This is clear later in the preface where the writers confess that their
work has been done only "after much consultation, not with flesh
and blood, but with his holy word."[6] Further, the preface argues
that the assembly's "care hath been to hold forth such things as are
of divine institution in every ordinance; and other things we have
endeavoured to set forth according to the rules of Christian prudence, agreeable to the general rules of the word of God."[7]

This faithfulness to the Puritan regulative principle of worship
is demonstrated further in the elements of worship that are then included. Only those matters which can be defended on the basis of
divine commands are included as acceptable parts of worship.
Hence, the Directory admits as legitimate worship the reading of
Scripture, prayer, preaching of the Word, and the proper administration of the sacraments. In accordance with divine limitations on
worship, responsive litanies, confirmation, godparents, kneeling
for communion, and the sign of the cross in baptism—all elements
contained in the Book of Common Prayer—are omitted in the
pertinent sections of the Directory. Only those activities which are
clearly commanded by God are given any warrant. Thus the Directory details the elements of worship that are considered substantial, or essential, in accordance with the Westminster
Confession of Faith, 1.6.

Other examples of omissions in the Directory are also illumi-
nating with regard to the practical application of the Puritan regulative principle of worship. No authorization of the use of the
ring in marriage is found.[8] The only music that is expressly authorized is the singing of Psalms, and the observance of any holy

day or festival is strictly forbidden.[9] The strict observance of the Sabbath alone is required.[10] Thus, there is clear agreement between the teaching of the Standards and the professed intent of the Directory.

A Compromise Document

As was true of the other assembly documents, the Directory was a compromise document.[11] With party views ranging from Erastian (state over church) to Independent Puritan to *jure divino* Presbyterian, anything other than a compromise document would have been impossible. Several significant aspects of its character as a compromise document are worthy of consideration.

First, the document was a compromise between the High Church elements and the free church elements. This is evident in several ways. To begin, the Directory is a book of recommendations, not a service book in the traditional sense.[12] It does not actually provide orders of worship but, rather, suggests possible actions and orders to be adapted to local custom and current needs. Further, the worship forms of the Directory are recommended as examples, not imposed as standard or uniform liturgies.[13] The preface to the Directory makes it clear that there was to be freedom in the use of its liturgical forms.[14] Therefore, allowance was made for the Scottish church to continue to use either its hallowed Knoxian Book of Common Order or the newer Directory. More specifically, the assembly was able to tread a middle path between the more radical Independents, the more conservative Scots (who were accustomed to the use of a service book), and the English Presbyterians (some of whom had high regard for the Prayer Book).

Robert Baillie, one of the Scots commissioners to Westminster, describes the tension between the English radicals and English conservatives encountered by the committee over this issue:

After, with huge deall of adoe, we had past the parts that concerned prayers, reading of Scripture, preaching, both the sacraments, ordination, and sanctification of the Sabbath, there was many references to the preface; and in this piece we expected most difficulty; one party purposing by the preface to turn the Directorie to a straight Liturgie; the other to make it so loose and free, that it should serve for little use: but God helped us to get both these rocks eschewed.[15]

In allowing the use of either the Book of Common Order or the Directory, and in granting freedom to use the forms as patterns or as set liturgies, the assembly achieved a significant development in terms of both freedom from coercion and freedom from liturgical conformity.

Second, there was compromise with regard to the guidelines for prayer. No absolute restriction was made regarding the use of free prayer or prescribed prayer. Free prayer is allowed, but there is no prohibition against written prayers, a major object of criticism among the stricter Puritans. It is important to note that the model prayers suggested by the Directory lend themselves to church use with only minor modification in phraseology. This is consistent with the Directory's expressed intent of providing the minister "some help and furniture" for the proper worship of God.[16] The prayer before the sermon is given with the notation that the order is but a "convenient order," which may be altered at the minister's discretion.[17] Likewise, the prayer after the sermon includes the reminder that the minister has freedom in the "manner" in which he prays, and that "he is left to his liberty, as God shall direct and enable him in piety and wisdom to discharge his duty."[18]

Third, it was necessary to reach a compromise over the use of particular forms of worship. For the Puritans, especially the Independents, many particulars, so-called novations,[19] of Scottish worship were unacceptable. "By these 'novations' the use of 'read prayers' and even of the Lord's Prayer, in public worship, was discountenanced, as was also the use of the Gloria Patri, and of the Apostles' Creed in the administration of the sacraments, and the habit of the minister to bow in silent prayer upon entering the pulpit."[20] The compromise that resulted neither prescribed the use of these particulars of worship (to the satisfaction of the Independents) nor proscribed their use (to the satisfaction of the Scottish Presbyterians).[21]

Fourth, and most important, a potentially explosive disagreement developed over the correct method of conducting the Lord's Supper.[22] The Scots were unable to understand the practice of the Independents, who conducted the Supper at every Sabbath gathering.[23] The English Independents could not understand the Scots' insistence that every communicant must sit around the table and were adamant for their own communion custom. Baillie complained that "the Independents, and all, loves so well sundry of their English guyses."[24] Eventually, compromises were reached, allowing the church session to determine the frequency of communion, and leaving room for the English and the Scots to follow their own customs in gathering for communion and distributing the elements.[25]

Further areas of compromise included, for example, the directions on providing funeral sermons, which were customary among the moderate English, but unacceptable to the Scots and English Independents. A formula was achieved granting liberty to offer the sermon.[26] On similar grounds, the Scots and English Independents disagreed over the propriety of including marriage as an ordinance of the church. Again, a middle path of liberty was pursued.[27] On another issue, concerning the propriety of nonministers publicly reading the Scriptures, division occurred between English Presbyterians, who contended that only the minister should read the Scriptures, and the Scots, who were accustomed to the office of reader in the Kirk. The Scots won a mild concession with the provision that candidates for the ministry might assist the pastor in reading the Scriptures.[28] A difference occurred over the question of having a sermon on Christmas Day, the Scots observing no festival days and the English yet holding to tradition and observing the day.[29]

The resulting Directory was a document that walked a middle path, a *via media*, among the extremes represented by the various parties of the Westminster Assembly. As such it was not everything that any one group desired but, rather, was sufficiently imprecise at crucial points to allow each his own interpretation.[30] This catholicity is at once a great strength and a great weakness of the Directory; for in the willingness to accommodate the diverse positions represented, the Directory further confused the already ambiguous distinction between essential and circumstantial aspects of worship.

DISCONTINUITY WITH THE WESTMINSTER STANDARDS

The one area of difference between the Westminster Standards and the Directory concerns matters of indifference, or *adiaphora*. The Standards see worship in terms of black and white only and leave no allowance for disputed matters in worship. That is, for the Westminster Confession of Faith and the Larger Catechism, unless a particular element of worship can appeal to direct biblical warrant, it has no justification and is no part of true biblical worship. But for the Directory, allowance is made for certain *circumstances* in worship, *adiaphora*, that were considered by some to be *elements* of worship!

The Directory is in agreement with the Westminster Standards on the necessity of biblical commands for all elements of worship, but in deference to the Scots it refrained from proscribing certain practices (the Doxology, the Creed, etc.) which otherwise fell under the Puritan ban. Likewise, in consideration of the Independents, no requirement was made in regard to certain questionable matters they preferred.

Therein lies the problem. While it may be possible to dismiss questions over the manner of observing communion as merely circumstances of worship, the problem is much more acute with other parts of worship, such as the Apostles' Creed, the Gloria, or the Doxology. Some regarded these as mere matters of circumstance. For others, they were elements. Likewise, to permit the hallowing of marriage, or the preaching of a funeral sermon, is to make room for what some regarded as elements of worship that are not strictly required, nor necessarily the logical consequences of any divine command. The documents of the Westminster Assembly uniformly assigned *adiaphora* only to the realm of the circumstantial—and a very narrow realm at that. Yet, as we have seen, numerous compromises were made over parts of worship that were regarded by the different parties as elements and not circumstances.

The problem, then, involves the difficult task of clearly delineating between essential matters of worship and merely circumstantial matters, a task made all the more difficult by constricting *adiaphora* and thus narrowing the range of circumstances. For the English Puritan, the use of the Apostles' Creed constituted, essentially, an element of worship and was accordingly condemned. For the Scottish Presbyterian, it was merely a circumstance of worship, an *adiaphoron*, and therefore acceptable. The black and white categories of the Standards allow no room for the maneuvering that was necessary to reach agreement in the Directory. Clearly, the Directory was not nearly as bold in the practical application of the Puritan regulative principle of worship as the later Westminster Confession of Faith was in its statement of the theory.

There is no clear explanation for the strict position of the Standards vis-à-vis the compromise character of the earlier Directory. A possible explanation is that the assembly felt free to embrace the strict interpretation in the Westminster Confession of Faith and the Larger Catechism because due allowance for the Scots had already been made in the Directory.[31] While this discontinuity with the

Standards does not constitute a license for liturgical experimentation, it nonetheless indicates that even at the inception, the Directory recognized that the application of the Puritan regulative principle of worship involved substantial practical difficulties.[32]

For the authors of the Directory to have stated (by an explicit series of prohibitions or requirements) the strict application of the principle in these disputed matters would have been to alienate and lose the support of one or more of the parties present.[33] On these disputed matters, the silence of the Directory speaks most eloquently. Significantly, this early minor compromise between Puritan theory and Presbyterian practice is indicative of ongoing tensions that would continue to arise in the history of Presbyterian worship. Such compromise virtually guaranteed that the church would experience controversy when applying the Puritan regulative principle of worship to issues of the day. It also indicates the need to broaden the definition of circumstances to include an expanded understanding of *adiaphora.*

Mitchell's analysis of the Directory is an apt summary of the major concerns of the document:

> I know of no formulary of the same sort which is so free from minute and harassing regulations as to postures, gestures, dresses, church pomp, ceremonies, symbolism, and other "superfluities," as Hales terms them, which "under pretext of order and decency" had crept into the church and more and more had restricted the liberty and burdened the consciences of its ministers. I know of none in which, throughout, so clear a distinction is kept up between what Christ and his apostles have instituted, and which may be regarded as imperative in Christian worship, and what has been authorised or recommended or permitted, under the rules of Christian prudence, by later and fallible church authorities, and the observance of which therefore is to be required or recommended or allowed, if at all, with greater

reserve as well as with more consideration for the scruples even of weaker brethren.[34]

It may be fair to say that the Directory is as consistent with the Westminster Standards as is practically possible. The Directory differs with the Standards only in the realization that a document that must encompass historic Presbyterian practices in worship, as well as contemporary free church concerns, could not press the Puritan regulative principle of worship to its logical conclusions, and at the same time attempt to provide a basis for unity. As far as the Directory was concerned, the majority of the assembly determined that it was better to bend the practical application of the regulative principle than to risk schism in the church.

SUMMARY

The foregoing analysis of the Westminster Standards and the Directory has demonstrated that the practical application of the Puritan regulative principle of worship, even by the Westminster Assembly itself, was not consistent with the theoretical formulation of the principle. If it was not possible for the Westminster Assembly to act consistently with its own definition of the regulative principle, there is little wonder that historic Presbyterian worship and contemporary Presbyterian practice find it impossible to follow the principle with consistency. The current liturgical confusion was virtually guaranteed from the start. Today's problem is indeed an old problem.

To summarize our findings thus far, the Puritan regulative principle of worship finds its proper historical context in the seventeenth century, as the ripe fruit of a century of Puritan thought, conceived and nurtured in opposition to the twin challenges of medieval Roman Catholicism and Reformation Anglicanism. The Puritan regulative principle consists of two parts. First, there is an affirmation that the *elements* of worship are regulated by Scripture, so that only what has been divinely instituted, commanded, or appointed (or the necessary logical corollary of what has been divinely instituted, commanded, or appointed) constitutes acceptable worship. Nonessential matters, or *circumstances*, are subject to the general teachings of Scripture and the proper exercise of common sense and Christian prudence. Second, there is a denial that the church and the state have the right to impose anything on the conscience of a believer that is contrary to the Word of God. Furthermore, "in matters of faith and worship," they do not even possess the right to require things that are not contrary to the Word. It is enough of an offense that their requirements go beyond the requirements of the Word of God.

In terms of the historic Anglican-Puritan controversies, the documents of the Westminster Assembly avoid some of the more pointed criticisms of Church of England practices. The Directory, for example, was only a recommended liturgy. Although adopted for use by the Church of England, it was a pattern for worship and avoided the imposition of *adiaphora*, or indifferent matters, on the consciences of individuals. Moreover, with regard to the Church of Scotland, it avoided the severe application of the Puritan regulative principle of worship, thus allowing for diversity of practice in matters deemed indifferent, but useful, by the Scots.

With the historical context before us, and a complete definition of the Puritan regulative principle of worship in mind, we may now move on to other related questions. To that end we will continue the investigation of the Puritan regulative principle of worship by way of a most important comparison, namely, by examining the relationship between the Puritan formulation and the teachings of John Calvin on true and proper worship.

Chapter 4

REGULATING WITH CALVIN

revious chapters have provided the necessary data to define precisely the nature of the Puritan regulative principle of worship. At this point, further investigation is needed in order to establish the relationship between John Calvin and later Calvinists, particularly the English Puritans of the seventeenth century. There is no disputing that the Puritans considered themselves to be heirs of Calvin and faithful conveyors of the great Reformer's thought. The degree to which they actually achieved this, however, is subject to some dispute.

The traditional view of the Puritans understood them to be faithful transmitters of the Genevan Reformation. Certainly there are differences of emphasis and structure between Calvin and his heirs. However, the traditional view explains these as a result of the diverse historical circumstances in which they labored and attributes their theological differences to an organic development in theology that occurred naturally. Thus, the traditional view underscores continuity in theological development from Calvin to Westminster, attributing any differences to natural, logical development.

In the 1970s and 1980s some scholars began to rethink the relationship between Calvin and his Puritan heirs. They argued that the relationship between them was explained best as a paradigm shift and not an organic development. Such discussions tended to focus on the role of covenant, the relation of faith to assurance, and the extent of the atonement. However, in spite of a number of works on worship, no single work has attempted to examine the relationship between Calvin's regulation of worship and the Puritan regulative principle.

In order to investigate Calvin's thought, it will be necessary to consider key passages in which he expressed his ideas on the regulation of worship and related issues. This consideration will move in two different, though related directions. First, we will consider in some detail Calvin's doctrine of the Word. Second, in light of Calvin's doctrine of the Word, we will look at his understanding of *adiaphora*, those matters not addressed directly in the Word.

Our sources will primarily be Calvin's own writings. Of course, his most important literary production was the *Institutes of the Christian Religion*.[1] This will be supplemented as needed by Calvin's commentaries and other writings, including sermons, letters, monographs, and liturgical rites. By establishing clearly Calvin's views on the Word and *adiaphora*, we will make significant progress toward understanding his regulation of worship. This will in turn provide the insight needed for a proper evaluation of the Puritan regulative principle of worship.

WORSHIP AND THE WORD OF GOD

In order to discuss Calvin's use of the Word of God, particularly its role in worship, it will be necessary to consider several important concepts. These may be categorized as (1) the authority of the Word in general, (2) the authority of the Word in worship, (3) the authority of the church vis-à-vis the authority of the Word, and (4) the proper method of interpreting the Word. These will be considered in order.

Although the 1536 edition of the *Institutes* contains scattered references to the Word of God, it does not have as full a discussion of the Scriptures as the definitive 1559 edition does. In the 1559 edition, there are three major sections that discuss the Word, but our concern is with two sections only. In book 1, chapters 6–9, Calvin discusses the Word in terms of our knowledge of God. In book 4, chapter 8, Calvin discusses the Word in relation to the authority of the church. These sections will be surveyed briefly, along with important passages from his sermons and commentaries, to determine Calvin's teaching on the authority of the Word. In addition, we shall make substantial use of several secondary sources for our investigation.

The Authority of the Word

For Calvin, there is a basic reason why Scripture is necessary. Although God has clearly displayed his power and majesty in creation, humanity would nevertheless be without a knowledge of salvation except for the Word, which Calvin terms another and better help (*ICR*, 1.6.1). Indeed, it was necessary that God be known as Redeemer as well as Creator (*ICR*, 1.6.2). Calvin extends the scope of Scripture beyond the knowledge of God, to include all doctrinal truth. "Now, in order that true religion may shine upon us, we ought to hold that it must take its beginning from heavenly doctrine and that no one can get even the slightest taste of right and sound doctrine unless he be a pupil of Scripture" (*ICR*, 1.6.2). The Scriptures are "spectacles" through which all other knowledge of God is viewed correctly (*ICR*, 1.6.1). Thus, all true knowledge about religion is confirmed by the Word. Ronald Wallace explains Calvin's view: "If we wish to know of Jesus Christ, and to bear witness to Him, it is to this source in the written word that we must turn, both for our necessary knowledge of the historical facts and for our understanding of the meaning of these facts."[2]

This revelation does not come from human sources, but from God. "Now daily oracles are not sent from heaven, for it pleased the Lord to hallow his truth to everlasting remembrance in the Scriptures alone [cf. John 5:39]. Hence the Scriptures obtain full authority among believers only when men regard them as having sprung from heaven as if there the living words of God were heard" (*ICR*, 1.7.1). For Calvin, this Word is "the eternal and inviolable truth of God." Although there has been much discussion of this matter in recent scholarship, there is no reason to doubt that for Calvin, the truth of God's Word demands that it be without error. As Robert Godfrey has stated it, "Calvin believed that every word of the Bible was God's Word and that every word was true in all that it says."[3] Further, Calvin teaches that the Scriptures serve as an adequate revelation of everything a person needs to know to attain salvation and to live a holy life.[4] Thus, for Calvin, the Word is absolutely authoritative in bringing to men and women the knowledge of God and his will.

The Authority of the Word in Worship

If for Calvin the Word of God is authoritative for all of life, then it is no great leap in logic to conclude that it is authoritative for matters of worship as well. Indeed, that is the case. In several key texts, Calvin vigorously asserts the definitive role of the Scriptures in determining the theory and practice of worship. In his sermon on Deuteronomy 5:8–10, he expounds the role of Scripture and notes two things in particular regarding the Word and worship. First, the Word must lead us because of our own sin and our propensity to idolatry. We would be unable to worship God purely unless God told us how we should properly worship and serve him. Calvin comments, with regard to our own intention in worship, that God "despises it and considers it detestable."[5] As Thomas Torrance has expressed it, "man must learn to serve God *against his own nature.*"[6] Second, God is pleased with our obedience to his commands. Thus, "we are to follow in all simplicity what he has ordained by his Word, without adding anything to it at all."[7] For Calvin, then, the only way to guarantee legitimate worship is to obey the commands of the Word.

He makes similar comments elsewhere in his sermons on Deuteronomy. While preaching on 4:23–26, Calvin makes several important points. Noting that God forbids all superstitious worship of idols and images, Calvin says it is normal "to mark out some one kind of superstition, thereby to warn us that we must keep ourselves from all superstitions in general" and that "we must hold ourselves in the simplicity of his word, without mingling any superstition with it."[8] Likewise, in his sermon on 11:5–8, Calvin comments on verse 8, "You see that the way for God's word to have due preeminence and authority among us, is that we govern not ourselves after our own liking, but hearken to the voice of Jesus Christ to submit ourselves thereto."[9] Thus, for Calvin, acceptable worship is that which is conformed to the Word of God and not the product of human invention.[10]

The Authority of the Church/Word

The question of the authority of the church is closely related to the Word and worship. In the 1536 edition of the *Institutes* we find a simple structure of six chapters: The first three are positive expositions of the Decalogue, the Apostles' Creed, and the Lord's Prayer, respectively. The last chapters are of a polemical nature, examining the true nature of sacraments, the spurious sacraments, and finally the nature of Christian freedom and the related problem of ecclesial and civil power.[11] It is in the last chapter that Calvin addresses the nature of true worship and begins to define the authority of the church. Benjamin Milner explains, "The word then, i.e., the Bible, serves as a legal code, obedience to the commandments and prohibitions of which constitutes the only acceptable worship, bearing in mind, of course, the changes which have been introduced by the coming of Christ."[12]

Calvin rejects the idea that the church has the right to formulate its own requirements for faith (*ICR*, 1536, 189). The application this has to the question of legitimate worship is clear. The Roman church had assumed her own infallibility, and required adherents to hear her pronouncements as binding—even as the Scriptures. Calvin agrees that we must listen when the church speaks. However, he limits the circumstances when the church may speak authoritatively (*ICR*, 1536, 194):

> The reason is that the church makes no pronouncement except from the Lord's Word. If they require anything more, let them know that these words of Christ afford them no support. . . . But is this "to be gathered in Christ's name" when God's commandment is cast aside that forbids anything to be added or taken away from his word [Deut. 4:2; cf. Deut. 12:32; Prov. 30:6; Rev. 22:18–19], anything to be ordained according to their own decision?

The same emphasis is found in an expanded form in book 4, chapters 8–10, of the 1559 edition of the *Institutes*. There Calvin picks up his theme that the church must speak in accordance with the Word of God (*ICR*, 4.8.13). He notes that "God deprives men of the capacity to put forth new doctrine in order that he alone may be our schoolmaster in spiritual doctrine as he alone is true" (*ICR*, 4.8.9). Calvin clarifies this, explaining that the authority of the church is "not infinite but subject to the Lord's Word" (*ICR*, 4.8.4). Further, the church cannot claim the leading of God's Spirit to sanction anything contrary to the Word, for the Spirit always agrees with the Word (*ICR*, 4.8.13). Neither can the officers of the church transgress the boundaries of God's Word. "In short, whatever authority is exercised in the Church ought to be subjected to this rule—that God's law is to retain its own pre-eminence, and that men blend nothing of their own, but only define what is right according to the Word of the Lord."[13] Certainly, the church has authority, but only under the higher authority of the Word.

Calvin's Interpretive Method

For Calvin, the ability to interpret aright is an essential element of the Reformed faith.[14] A complete discussion of Calvin's interpretive method (hermeneutics) would be worthy of investigation in its own right. Here we can do no more than consider two closely related aspects of Calvin's biblical interpretation—namely, his use of the analogy of faith and the principle of contextualization—and consider their applications to the regulation of worship.

The analogy of faith includes the idea that the interpretation of a difficult passage is always made in the light of clearer texts. However, it goes beyond the analogy of Scripture in that it also considers the overall theological teaching of Scripture.[15] The principle of contextualization means that Calvin is not interested in a bare exegesis of the passage, but seeks to determine the circumstances and occasion of the text in order to gain insight into its true intent. Calvin unites these twin concerns against a hermeneutic that would lift words out of context, appealing to their meaning without regard to occasion, rhetorical device, or conformity to the rest of Scripture.

Calvin explains these concerns in his comments on the meaning of the Ten Commandments. Complaining about those who limit the meaning of the text to the words only, Calvin says, "The commandments and prohibitions always contain more than is expressed in words." Or, as he says further in the passage, "Therefore, plainly a sober interpretation of the law goes beyond the words" (*ICR*, 2.8.8).[16] Similarly, Calvin argues that we must seek to determine the reason a particular command was given. Thus, for Calvin, a true method of interpretation will focus, not just on the bare literal meaning of the text, but on the overall teaching of the passage. H. W. Rossouw observes that Calvin avoids both a biblicistic approach and an extreme confessional usage of the analogy of faith.[17] In other words, Calvin embraced neither the unbridled, individualistic literalism of the Anabaptists, nor the "party-line," magisterial interpretation of the Roman Catholic Church.[18]

Donald McKim has explained Calvin's concerns: "His studies in legal exegesis showed him that the intent of the author is more important than the etymology of words."[19] Calvin called the latter emphasis "syllable-snatching" (*ICR*, 4.17.23). For example, he rejected the Anabaptist view that Christ's prescription in the Sermon on the Mount, "Do not swear at all" (Matt. 5:34), prohibits all oath taking. Calvin said, "Here, however, we shall never attain the truth unless we fix our eyes upon Christ's intention and give heed to what he is driving at in that passage" (*ICR*, 2.8.26).

A similar observation has been made by Bernard Zylstra. Approaching the question of interpretive method theologically, Zylstra points out that a true hermeneutical approach must be "covenantal," thus seeking to relate the particulars to the overall unity of Scripture and man's responsibility to God. Attacking the approach that would interpret portions of Scripture in isolation from the remainder of Scripture, Zylstra says,

> The point is that rationalistic propositionalism operates with a conception of truth that may stem from Aristotle or positivism, but not from the Bible itself. *For truth in the Scriptures is covenantal, referring to the entire context of God's dealing with man.* For this reason, a single text, or a chapter, or even an entire book of the Bible contains truth that can only be understood *in that entire context.* The final context is Christ, the Word through Whom all things were made, and the Word made flesh through Whom God is making all things new. Christ is therefore the key to the Scriptures; without Him they remain a closed book.[20]

Another way to describe Calvin's interpretive method would be to contrast the terms "relative" and "absolute." An "absolute" interpretation of a given passage would take the meaning of the passage as it appears, with its full force, and with little regard for harmonizing it with the overall teaching of Scripture. Thus a prohibition against oaths becomes an absolute prohibition of oaths under all circumstances. Ben Farley has observed that this literalism regarding the oath is one of Calvin's strongest complaints about the Anabaptists.[21] Here Farley notes that, for Calvin, a passage must be understood "relatively." That is, it must be related to the immediate occasion and circumstances, to the immediate context, to the overall teaching of the particular book, and ultimately must conform with the overall theological context of Scripture.[22]

The importance of the distinction between "absolute" and "relative" interpretation is critical, for in it lies our hope of harmonizing Calvin's strong prohibitions against adding to the Word with his high regard for practices of the primitive church that are clearly postapostolic. For example, we must find a way to reconcile Calvin's unwavering commitment to Scripture as authoritative with his high regard for the rite of confirmation. Our other option is simply to conclude that Calvin was hopelessly and foolishly inconsistent! That option is not appealing at all.

Somehow, then, priorities and relationships must be established between the absolute authority of the Word and the subordinate authority of the church. Similarly, a balance must be maintained between the teaching of individual texts and their relationship to the overall teaching of the Scriptures and the pedagogical needs of the church. For Calvin, simple, mechanical answers are inadequate responses to God's provision of the Word and the church. Rather, thoughtful and serious efforts at interpretation must be made, always keeping in mind the normative role of the Word, the covenantal context in which the Word is revealed, and the subordinate, but necessary values and roles of tradition and pedagogy.

THE ROLE OF ADIAPHORA

In addition to the interpretive keys discussed above, the role of *adiaphora,* or indifferent things, is critical in the regulation of worship. *Adiaphora* may be defined further in order to clarify their content and scope. "Philosophical, ethical, and theological writers recognize that things indifferent are of three major types. There are ceremonial *adiaphora*—rites, ceremonies, and customs that in themselves are neither commanded nor prohibited. There are ethical *adiaphora*—acts and habits, such as drinking wine, that in themselves can be committed or omitted without fault. There are doctrinal *adiaphora*—doctrines that can be accepted or rejected, or of which a person may remain ignorant without sin."[23] For our purposes, the nature and legitimacy of doctrinal *adiaphora* are not under consideration. Ethical and ceremonial *adiaphora* are most relevant to this discussion.

Adiaphora and Christian Freedom

In the 1536 edition of the *Institutes*, Calvin places the discussion of *adiaphora* in the context of Christian freedom. For Calvin, there are three parts to Christian freedom.[24] The first is based on justification by faith, namely, that we realize that our righteousness does not depend on our works, but on the completed work of Christ, which frees us from the power of the law (*ICR*, 1536, 176). The second is closely related to the first. The believer is obedient to the law, not "as if constrained by the necessity of the law," but rather in joyful submission to the Lord in response to God's free justification (*ICR*, 1536, 177). The third brings the reader to the context of the discussion of *adiaphora*. Calvin explains, "The third part of Christian freedom is that we are bound before God by no religious obligation to outward things of themselves 'indifferent'; but are permitted sometimes to use them, sometimes to leave them, indifferently" (*ICR*, 1536, 179). Here, in regard to matters in the church—not necessary to salvation—Calvin asserts the principle of indifference.[25] Thus one is free to use or abstain from using those things neither commanded nor forbidden.

As the discussion continues, it is apparent that Calvin is primarily concerned with ethical *adiaphora*. However, ceremonial *adi-*

aphora are present as well.[26] Calvin has said that there are some matters that in themselves may be viewed as indifferent or morally neutral. He notes a few of the things that he considers indifferent. "Today we seem to many to be unreasonable because we stir up discussion over the unrestricted eating of meat, use of holidays and of vestments, and similar vain frivolities (as it seems to them)" (*ICR*, 1536, 179). What is important for Calvin is not the question, Are these matters addressed specifically in the Scriptures? He is not guilty of some minimalist method of prooftexting. On the contrary, as we established earlier, Calvin seeks conformity to the overall teaching of Scripture. Also, throughout his entire discussion, he is primarily concerned about the attitude of the worshiper, that it be one of submission and faithfulness to the Scriptures, God's revealed will.

Calvin's understanding of *adiaphora* may be described further. First, it is necessary that there be an awareness of the freedom, the *libertatis cognitio*, that the Christian possesses. This is in keeping with Calvin's emphasis on man's proximity to God's revelation and his responsibility to apprehend that knowledge for covenantal obedience. Second, there must be an avoidance of an overly scrupulous conscience, "for when consciences have once ensnared themselves, they enter a long and inextricable maze, not easy to get out of" (*ICR*, 1536, 179). Likewise, an extravagant or libertine use of freedom is to be avoided (*ICR*, 1536, 180). Thus, the wise Christian will learn to avoid the extremes of both scrupulosity and licentiousness and with "a clean conscience cleanly use God's gifts" (*ICR*, 1536, 180).

Third, things indifferent must be considered in conjunction with both Christian charity and Christian liberty (*ICR*, 1536, 181). Ronald Wallace explains Calvin's concern: "It is true that . . . there are occasions when we must refuse to express our liberty of conscience in outward behavior, lest we offend others within the Church. Yet even when we are subjecting the outward expression of our liberty of conscience to the law of charity, our consciences can at the same time remain free before God and unbound by our outward behavior."[27] This concern with charity and liberty leads, naturally enough, to the next major concern in Calvin's view of *adiaphora*, the role of conscience.

Conscience and Ceremony

It should be noted that Calvin's discussion of ethical *adiaphora* in the 1559 edition is practically identical with his work in the 1536 edition.[28] However, in the 1559 edition, he does add some important thoughts. To strengthen the idea that *adiaphora* and their use (determined by charity) must be subordinated to the teaching of the Scriptures, Calvin says, "For as our freedom must be subordinated to love, so in turn ought love itself to abide under purity of faith" (*ICR*, 3.19.13). Further additions may be found in book 3, chapter 19. In the second half of section 15 and all of section 16 Calvin expands the discussion to clarify (1) the requirements of civil government for obedience and (2) the voluntary curtailment of freedom for the sake of a brother. Calvin notes that the major problem between conscience (freedom) and the civil or voluntary curtailment of that freedom lies in the failure to make one key distinction. "The question, as I have said, is not of itself very obscure or involved. However, it troubles many because they do not sharply enough distinguish the outer forum, as it is called, and the forum of conscience" (*ICR*, 3.19.15).

Likewise, in his comments on 1 Corinthians 6:12, he says, "Every one has liberty inwardly in the sight of God on this condition, that all must restrict the use of their liberty with a view to mutual edification."[29] As he defines conscience, it is our witness before God regarding the thoughts and intents of the heart. For Calvin, then, it is the conscience that attests to integrity and freedom before God, even while the person is abstaining from freedom for the sake of other believers (*ICR*, 3.19.15).

One of the major changes in the 1559 edition of the *Institutes* is the addition of a large section devoted to ceremonial *adiaphora*.

This is found in the discussion of the power of the church, *Institutes*, book 4, chapter 10. Calvin begins his exposition of the role of conscience and the power of the church by referring to other cases of conscience. He notes the tension that arises between freedom of conscience and the right of the magistrate to exact obedience from his subjects (*ICR*, 4.10.3). Calvin's answer to this dilemma, as seen above, is in the appeal of the conscience before God.

Likewise, with regard to the concerns of a weaker brother, Calvin explains that "however necessary abstention may be to him with regard to his brother, as is prescribed by God, still he does not cease to retain freedom of conscience. We see that this law, binding only outward works, leaves the conscience free" (*ICR*, 4.10.4). Thus, freedom of conscience, while not unrelated to external circumstances, ultimately is decided *coram deo* (before God). This is important in its application to the power of the church, namely, that it frees the believer from the imposition of church laws or ceremonies that would bind the conscience (*ICR*, 4.10.6). Thus, no authority, whether civil or ecclesial, has the right to bind the conscience in matters that before God are free.

Guidelines for Determining Adiaphora

In *Institutes*, book 4, chapter 10, Calvin continues his discussion of conscience by providing guidelines that may be used to determine if ceremonies are legitimate.[30] The first guideline concerns the legitimate authority of the church in relation to the authority of God (sections 5–8). Here Calvin sets out the difference between the legitimate use of church power and the abuse of that power by Rome. He insists on maintaining the legitimate authority of the church but limits that authority to those who use it wisely and do not usurp the prerogatives of the Lord (*ICR*, 4.10.7). The reasons for this are twofold. First, the church does not have the authority to burden the believer with new laws or ceremonies that go beyond the requirements of Scripture. Calvin appeals to the apostle Paul, who "argues in the letter to the Colossians that we are not to seek from men the doctrine of the true worship of God, for the Lord has faithfully and fully instructed us how he is to be worshiped" (*ICR*, 4.10.8).

Second, in the same section Calvin argues that the authority of the Lord is such that only he has the right to mandate worship. To make a human requirement binding, even as a divine requirement is binding, is to violate the authority of God and unjustly to bind the conscience. As T. Watson Street explains it: "Liberty of conscience must not be destroyed by men. To do so is to invade the Kingdom of God—for conscience is subject to God alone. Therefore, men must not command anything, independent of the Word, as essentially necessary, or necessary to salvation or necessary for true piety."[31] Indeed, for Calvin, Jesus alone is able to judge in these matters.[32]

The second guideline concerns the nature of ceremonies, their legitimacy, and their limitation (sections 9–18). Aside from the basic denial of God's authority inherent in many papal requirements, Calvin makes two other criticisms. "First, they prescribe observances for the most part useless and sometimes even foolish; secondly, pious consciences are oppressed with an immense multitude of them, and reverting to a kind of Judaism, so cling to shadows that they cannot reach Christ" (*ICR*, 4.10.11). Does this, then, exclude all ceremonies? No, but there are certain limitations that must not be transgressed. There must be an avoidance of pomp (*ICR*, 4.10.12), a limit on the useless multiplication of ceremonies (*ICR*, 4.10.13), and a proper end for which the ceremonies are intended, namely, to show forth Christ (*ICR*, 4.10.14). Calvin sums up his concerns in these words:

> Shall no ceremonies then (you will ask) be given to the ignorant to help them in their inexperience? I do not say that. For I feel that this kind of help is very useful to them. I only contend that the means used ought to show Christ, not to

hide him. Therefore, God has given us a few ceremonies, not at all irksome, to show Christ present. To the Jews more were given as images of Christ absent. He was absent, I say, not in power, but in the means by which he might be made known. Accordingly, to keep that means, it is necessary to keep fewness in number, ease in observance, dignity in representation, which also includes clarity. [*ICR*, 4.10.14]

The third guideline picks up a theme that Calvin has pursued on several other occasions (sections 19–22). Here he argues against medieval Roman Catholic practices such as "these priestly vestments that we see in the Mass, these altar ornaments, these gesticulations, and the whole apparatus of useless things" (*ICR*, 4.10.19). Calvin's argument at this point, however, is not directed primarily against these particulars. Instead, he is again sounding the theme of the believer's conscience, its freedom from coercion, and the necessity of charity with regard to the weaker brother. That is, he argues here more against the act of imposition than against the thing that is imposed. For Calvin, "there is still a great deal of difference between establishing some exercise of piety which believers may use with a free conscience, or (if it will serve them no useful purpose) abstain from it, and making a law to entrap consciences in bondage" (*ICR*, 4.10.20). No ceremony, then, regardless of its roots in antiquity, is acceptable if it is imposed on the free conscience of believers as though it were a law of God. Such burdens are overwhelming.[33]

This does not mean that the church is unable to speak to the circumstances of the day. Indeed, it is permissible to prescribe a certain ceremony or rite as long as three conditions are met: (1) it must be framed according to love (for the sake of the weak); (2) it must not be viewed as an addition to God's law; and (3) it must be intended for a particular need at a particular time in the life of the church (*ICR*, 4.10.22). Where these conditions are met, it is possible to introduce a practice, a rite, or a ceremony, or to abstain from it as long as there is no imposition or coercion of the conscience.

The fourth guideline is found in sections 23–26. Here Calvin takes to task human innovations in worship as usurping the authority that God alone possesses (*ICR*, 4.10.23). This is a theme that resounds throughout Calvin's writings. For example, in commenting on the second commandment, Calvin says, "God is here set before us in the character of a husband, who suffers no rival; or if it be preferred to extend the meaning of the word, He is called the assertor of His rights; since His rivalry is nothing more than retaining what is His own."[34] Likewise, in his sermon on Deuteronomy 5:4–7, he argues for God's jealousy in worship, "for God cannot allow any rival."[35] For Calvin, it is impossible to worship God properly when that worship has been corrupted by human innovations. Instead of true humility, God is offered only a "sham obedience" (*ICR*, 4.10.24).

The final guideline is found in sections 27–32, where Calvin seeks to reconcile order and authority in the church with freedom of conscience. He admits the general rule that "some form of organization is necessary in all human society to foster the common peace and maintain concord" (*ICR*, 4.10.27). He goes on to explain that, in the church, there are two types of rules that are legitimate. The first seeks to establish order in the use of rites and ceremonies so that they are characterized by "modesty and gravity" (*ICR*, 4.10.28) and ultimately "lead us straight to Christ" (*ICR*, 4.10.29). Examples of this would include the proper physical position in prayer (kneeling), and the dignified manner in which the church administers the Lord's Supper. The second seeks to remove confusion and foster "discipline and peace" in the congregation. In this category, Calvin places such matters as the time and place of worship, reverence in worship, and any additional matters of church discipline (*ICR*, 4.10.29).[36]

Calvin addresses the hard question of conscience in reference to the rule of the church. How does one distinguish between what is legitimate and what is a usurpation of God's authority? First, the Lord himself has already spoken on every matter that is necessary for salvation. "Therefore in these the Master alone is to be heard" (*ICR*, 4.10.30). Second, God has not given an exact, detailed prescription of every aspect of worship. Thus, the church must rely on general rules or broader precepts from which specific applications must be made. Third, sensitivity must be exercised in the development of new practices or the abolition of old practices. As the church tries to adapt its practice of nonessentials to "the customs of each nation and age," it must not "charge into innovation rashly" but must be led by love (*ICR*, 4.10.30).

Calvin concludes by giving three general rules for the observance of ceremonies (*ICR*, 4.10.32): (1) the rules and observance should be kept to a minimum; (2) there should be no superstition where ceremonies are observed, and no contention where they are not; and (3) rites and ceremonies should always be contextualized to the time, place, and needs of the church. On the last point, Calvin says:

> We should refer the entire use and purpose of observances to the upbuilding of the church. If the church requires it, we may not only without any offense allow something to be changed but permit any observances previously in use among us to be abandoned. This present age offers proof of the fact that it may be a fitting thing to set aside, as may be opportune in the circumstances, certain rites that in other circumstances are not impious and indecorous. For (such was the blindness and ignorance of former times) churches have heretofore stuck fast in ceremonies with corrupt opinion and stubborn intent. Consequently, they can scarcely be sufficiently cleansed of frightful superstitions without removing many ceremonies probably established of old with good reason and not notably impious of themselves. [*ICR*, 4.10.32]

It is important to note that some of the *adiaphora* that Calvin would admit into the church perhaps stretch the category of "circumstances" of worship to the limit, but do not constitute substantial parts or elements of worship.

Street has summarized Calvin's teaching on *adiaphora* and the importance he placed on fidelity to the Scriptures:

> Calvin measured things indifferent by the Word of God. While discussing ceremonial or ethical *adiaphora* he used the teaching of Scripture to determine if the things in question were allowed. For things indifferent are those things about which the Scripture has no command or prohibition and which, therefore, God has left free. The Bible, then, is the criterion for things indifferent.[37]

For Calvin, whatever was in itself indifferent, and in its use in accord with the overall teaching of Scripture, was legitimate.

Now that we have determined Calvin's use of the Word and development of the concept of *adiaphora*, we must examine his application of the Word to questions of worship. What role do *adiaphora* play in Calvin's regulation of worship? How does Calvin's understanding of worship compare to that of his Puritan heirs? We turn now to these matters in the next chapter.

Chapter 5

WORSHIP, GENEVAN STYLE

*C*alvin's emphasis on Scripture provides a solid anchor for his teaching, a benchmark against which to evaluate all controversies. His concept of *adiaphora* provides a broad base for contextualizing worship to the needs of various times and places. However, these two emphases highlight a tension between Calvin and his heirs. There was considerable agreement among all Puritan parties that the Word of God was the sole authority in matters of faith and worship. Indeed, this served to unite them in their opposition to the Anglican establishment. However, this high view of the authority of Scripture was Calvin's professed belief as well. It is this purported agreement, along with differing views on *adiaphora*, that leads to the tension. For, as we shall see, there were substantial differences in practice between Calvin and the Puritans. Thus, the similarity in their professions regarding the Word of God makes their differences in worship all the more striking.

As noted by many historians, there was a spectrum of Puritan belief during the Elizabethan and Jacobean eras (1558–1625). During the time of James I, there were different degrees of nonconformity among the Presbyterians, Independents, and Separatists. However, in spite of differences among Puritans, Calvin's theory and practice of worship (which will be discussed below) clearly differed from all Puritans.

Practically, it should be remembered that these groups represented a wide range when it came to the degree of their agreement or disagreement with Calvin. The Separatists, most closely aligned with Baptist and Brownist sentiments, were the most critical of continental Calvinistic worship. The Presbyterians, still maintaining many traditional Calvinistic practices, were the most compatible with Calvin's views. The Independents represented a broad array of beliefs that encompassed, at times, the positions of the other two parties.

Further complicating this categorization is the fact that individuals within these general groupings occasionally violated specifics of their respective party themes. In light of this complicated situation, the discussion below is an attempt to address the issues that *generally* divide Calvin from all Puritans. The specific differences that will be examined may be categorized as differences over the shape of the liturgy and differences over the practice of worship.

THE SHAPE OF THE LITURGY

One of the most obvious differences in Calvin's understanding of worship and that of the later Puritans lies in the shape of the liturgy. For Calvin, the Lord's Supper was a matter of the greatest import. It was not an addendum to be tacked on occasionally to the sermon, but always should be coordinated with it. Ronald Wallace rightly notes that for Calvin, the Lord's Supper "should be *subordinated to the Word.*" This, however, is in perfect harmony with the assertion above because Calvin viewed the Word as more extensive than the sermon.[1] Indeed, borrowing from Augustine, he spoke of the Lord's Supper as a "visible word" (*ICR*, 4.14.6). Thus, in understanding Calvin's thinking, it is a grave error to replace the primacy of the Word with the primacy of preaching.

In regards to theory and practice, there are some clear differences between Calvin and the Puritans. Indeed, Calvin's balanced approach was superior to the heavily didactic worship of the Puritans. In Zurich, Zwingli based his liturgical model on the medieval *pronaus*, or "prone."[2] The prone was a brief preaching service inserted into the mass in the common language of the people, "consisting of a sermon, which was preceded or followed by the bidding of the bedes, notices, and instruction in the Decalogue, the Lord's Prayer, and similar formularies."[3]

Calvin, however, conceived of worship according to the model of the mass, which always included the liturgy of word and the table; in other terminology, the ante-communion and communion. Such a practice would have been most consistent with the practice of the primitive church, for which Calvin had high regard.[4] William Maxwell has aptly summarized Calvin's concerns: "To Calvin, the 'means of grace' were twofold, consisting of *both* the Word and the Sacraments. The Ministry was a ministry of the Word *and* the Sacraments. A minister's task and office was not only to preach and instruct, but also to celebrate the Lord's Supper every week, and to teach and urge the people to communicate weekly."[5]

Calvin clearly went on record for an every-week observance of the Lord's Supper as a minimum. Note his words in this regard: "The Supper could have been administered most becomingly if it were set before the church very often, and at least once a week" (*ICR*, 4.17.43).[6] His failure to convince the Genevan authorities to accept this practice (they opted for quarterly observance) should not detract from the great importance that frequent communion held in Calvin's thought.

From a biblical and historical perspective, Calvin considered frequent communion necessary to conform more nearly to the practice of the early church. Bard Thompson notes that Calvin's model was "the ancient church of the apostles, the martyrs, and the holy fathers."[7] More pointedly, James Jordan has observed that Calvin, along with many other Reformers, desired to return not simply to the New Testament, which was an Anabaptist concern, but rather to restore the ancient rites of the old catholic church.[8] As H. Jackson Forstman describes it, "Calvin not only is willing to accept, but also thinks all Christians should accept the decrees of the first four general councils, not because there is anything inherently sacred about those councils but rather because they 'contain nothing but the pure and natural interpretation of the Scripture.' "[9]

From a practical or pastoral perspective, Calvin recognized the need for addressing the nonrational aspect of humanity and maintaining redemption as a divine mystery.[10] Thus, to achieve balance in worship, the Supper was always to accompany the sermon. None of this is intended to say that the Puritans failed to honor the Lord's Supper when celebrated. Instead, the intent is to show that for Calvin, worship was incomplete without the Supper.

The Puritans did not conceive of the Supper as having this degree of importance. The Middleburg Liturgy, a product of the more advanced English Puritans, was published in 1586. It contained rubrics in the section on the Lord's Supper that communion observance "shalbe comonly once a moneth, or so ofte as the Congregation shall thinke expedient."[11] Likewise, the 1587 Puritan Book of Discipline, often attributed to Walter Travers, speaks of communion as occurring "every month."[12] The Westminster Directory encouraged "frequent" communion, but left the final decision determining the frequency in the hands of each congregation.[13]

Although the Independents at the assembly were accustomed to frequent, even weekly communion, the Presbyterians were accustomed to Knox's Book of Common Order, which stated the Lord's Supper "is used once a monthe," and the first Book of Discipline, which said, " 'foure tymes in the yeare' was 'sufficient.' "[14] Horton Davies observed that "it cannot be doubted that the Puritans did not follow the lead of Calvin in emphasizing the centrality and dignity of the Lord's Supper."[15] Thus, the Puritans differed with Calvin's view of the shape of the liturgy and the necessity of weekly observance for the sacrament of communion.

The Puritans differed with Calvin not only on the shape of the liturgy and the frequency of communion, but also in the particulars of observing the sacrament. Their objections lay in two areas specifically. Concerning the manner of reception, kneeling was anathematized by the Puritans.[16] In 1552 an incipient Puritanism had censured the second Edwardian prayer for prescribing kneeling at communion.[17] In order to accommodate the consciences of the objectors, the so-called Black Rubric was added explicitly to deny that kneeling should be understood as giving any support to the Roman Catholic doctrine of transubstantiation (i.e., kneeling was not to be interpreted as adoration of the host).[18]

For Calvin, the traditional practice of kneeling for communion was acceptable and not a matter for controversy.[19] The Westminster Directory did not specifically prohibit kneeling, but the intention of the text is clearly limited to the accepted English and Scottish practices of reception in the pew or around the table.[20] John Barkley points out that Presbyterian practice "had been for the minister and people to kneel for the prayer of consecration" and then assume their seats for observing communion.[21]

For Calvin, questions regarding the type of bread used, or the color of the wine, or even the manner of reception were all matters of complete indifference.

> But as for the outward ceremony of the action—whether or not the believers take it in their hands, or divide it among themselves, or severally eat what has been given to each; whether they hand the cup back to the deacon or give it to the next person; whether the bread is leavened or unleav-

ened; the wine red or white—it makes no difference. These things are indifferent and left at the church's discretion. [*ICR*, 4.17.43]

In fact, Calvin used both leavened and unleavened bread in communion. He accommodated himself to the Genevan practice of using leavened bread during his first stay.[22] Later, after Geneva conformed to some of the practices of the church in Bern, Calvin with good conscience used the unleavened wafer.[23]

In a departure from the tolerant spirit of their mentor, the Puritans rejected Calvin's practice concerning the elements used in communion. They opposed the use of the wafer, insisting instead on the use of common (leavened) bread.[24] In the Edwardian prayer books, a significant change occurred between 1549 and 1552. In the 1549 prayer book, the rubrics on communion included instructions that "the bread prepared for the Communion be made, through all this realm, after one sort and fashion: that is to say, unleavened, and round, as it was afore, but without all manner of print, and something more larger and thicker than it was."[25] However, in the 1552 prayer book, the instructions called for bread "as is usual to be eaten at the table . . . the best and purest wheat bread."[26] This was in accordance with the Puritan effort to distance the Church of England from Roman Catholic practice.

More explicitly, in the 1572 Admonition to Parliament, the anonymous author(s) contrasted the Anglican practice, which reverted in 1560 to the use of the unleavened wafer, with the practice of the early church.[27] "Then they ministered the Sacrament with common and usual bread: now with wafer cakes, brought in by Pope Alexander, being in form, fashion, and substance, like their god of the altar."[28] The unleavened wafer, then, failed the biblical requirement of being a "common loaf" and was viewed as unsuitable for worship. Again, the Puritans departed from the regulation of worship as understood by Calvin. For Calvin, these were matters of indifference, to be determined by the needs of the

church, expediency, and decorum. To make an issue over the use
of the wafer would be a frivolous indulgence.

THE PRACTICE OF WORSHIP

Another significant area of difference lies in the manner in
which Calvin and the Puritans regarded the practice of worship in
general and the various parts of worship in particular. This may be
further categorized into differences over (1) the use of formal liturgical worship, (2) the role of ceremony, and (3) the propriety of
certain traditional acts of worship. These are very complicated
matters, but some direction is possible. Each of these will be surveyed to determine Calvin's view, and a brief outline of the con-
trasting Puritan view will be offered. This comparison will provide
greater understanding of the differences between Calvin and his
Puritan heirs.

The Use of Liturgies

As should be expected, the more consistent Puritans had little
regard for the use of formal liturgies; but this is not true of all Puritans, for some did not oppose liturgical worship per se. Nevertheless, many objected to formal liturgies with set prayers and
responses, for more reasons than a simple objection to their imposition. Certainly this is true of the earlier Puritans as well as later,
more moderate Puritans—even into the period of the Westminster
Assembly. Eventually, the various parties reached a compromise at
the time of the Westminster Assembly, resulting in the production
of a compromise Directory with no representative forms for use in
worship. Instead, the Westminster Directory is not a service book
per se, but a book of instructions or "help and furniture" in worship.[29]

For Calvin, a structured liturgy provided in a service book was
not a wicked substitute for genuine religious affection.[30] On the

contrary, it was a means for instructing the congregation and avoiding the temptation to innovations that would undermine the direct, simple worship of the early church.[31] He explained his thinking in a letter to the Protector Somerset in 1548.

> Indeed, I do not say that it may not be well, and even necessary, to bind down the pastors and curates to a certain written form, as well for the sake of supplementing the ignorance and deficiencies of some, as the better to manifest the conformity and agreement between all the churches; . . . to take away all ground of pretence for bringing in any eccentricity or new-fangled doctrine on the part of those who only seek to indulge an idle fancy; as I have already said, the Catechism ought to serve as a check upon such people. There is, besides, the form and manner of administration of the sacraments; also the public prayers.[32]

For these reasons, Calvin had developed set forms of worship for use both in Strasbourg and in Geneva.[33]

Contrast this with the Westminster Directory, which makes no attempt at providing a set liturgy but, rather, suggests representative forms of prayer. Of course, Calvin saw the need for some extemporaneous prayers, and made provision for them.[34] Nevertheless, he felt that sound pedagogical considerations were at stake in the use of set prayers. Likewise, uniformity in prayer was helpful, given the present state of ministerial abilities. Calvin's overall balance in this regard provides a sharp contrast to the narrower approach of the Puritans. In fact, even Knox (with his strong views on reform) favored the use of a service book, although he specifically objected to the use of the 1552 prayer book.[35]

The Role of Ceremony

If, however, the Puritans were somewhat divided over the question of liturgy, there was much greater agreement in their opposition to ceremony. For Calvin, a number of items were acceptable that the Puritans adamantly opposed. These items of ceremony included the use of godparents in the baptism of infants, the use of distinctive ministerial garb, the observance of days, the practice of confirmation, and the use of certain forms of worship.

For example, in the rite of infant baptism, Calvin continued the traditional practice of using godparents as sponsors. In the Ecclesiastical Ordinances of Geneva, the basis of church discipline during Calvin's second Genevan ministry, the following guideline is stated: "Strangers are not to be accepted as godparents but only Christian persons who are also members of our own communion, since others are not capable of promising the Church to instruct the children as they should."[36] Interestingly enough, Maxwell provides citations from the register of the English congregation in Geneva that list both John Calvin and John Knox as godparents![37] Calvin further clarifies the use of godparents in the Ordinances for Supervision of Churches in the Country: "No godfather is to be admitted for presenting a child, unless he is of an age to make such a promise; that is, he must have passed fifteen years, be of the same confession as ourselves, and be duly instructed."[38]

For the Puritans, this was a nonbiblical practice and therefore not allowed.[39] The Church of England was familiar with the role of godparents, having explicit statements in the various prayer books that indicated their responsibilities. These rubrics also demonstrate the similarity between the Genevan and Anglican practice. After professing faith on behalf of the baptized infant, godparents were exhorted, "You must remember that it is your parts and duties to see that these infants be taught, so soon as they shall be able to learn, what a solemn vow, promise, and profession they have made by you."[40] Thus, both Geneva and England required promises by the godparents on behalf of the infants to instruct those infants in the Christian faith.

No provision is made in the Westminster Directory, however, for the role of godparents in the section "Of the Administration of the Sacraments: and first, of baptism." More explicitly, the 1661 Exceptions against the Book of Common Prayer seeks relief from required conformity to this practice.[41] Calvin, on the other hand, saw this as a matter of indifference, neither commanded nor forbidden. Therefore, on the grounds that it was useful to the edification of the church, and its use was consistent with biblical teaching, Calvin continued its practice.[42]

A second issue of ceremony is that of the clothing of the minister. The practice of the Roman Catholic Church had been to clothe the priest in the alb, chasuble, stole, and surplice. The Puritan response to Reformation in England was to seek the removal of all ecclesiastical garb as a violation of the regulative principle. While Calvin gave no evidence of fondness for vestments and indeed displayed some dislike of them, his attitude was quite different from that of the Puritans. At this point, Calvin's view was largely representative of the continental Reformed.[43] In a letter to Heinrich Bullinger, he makes mention of John Hooper's imprisonment over the question of vestments and comments: "I had rather he had not carried his opposition so far with respect to the cap and the linen vestment, even although I do not approve of these."[44]

The practice in Geneva was the use of the black gown, the so-called Geneva gown. This gown, which was the usual outdoor dress of the priest, was not a part of the vestments for worship, but was recognized as the distinctive garb of the minister.[45] The Puritan abhorrence of distinctive dress brought results that were most curious. "On the one hand the refusal to wear vestments was carried to the conclusion of rejecting any distinctive ministerial dress; on the other hand churches had developed their own 'Reformed' attire, enforced by congregational opinion."[46] Again, the Puritans were far removed from Calvin's attitude of (begrudging) tolerance with regard to vestments and his acceptance of the Genevan attire as the customary garb of the Reformed minister.

A third issue of ceremony over which Calvin and the Puritans differed is the question of the observance of days. This issue may be approached from two perspectives. First, Calvin was not a sabbatarian and therefore did not consider Sunday observance, the Lord's Day, to require the strict regulation that the Puritans later held so dear. For Calvin, the Sabbath had been fulfilled in Christ in terms of ceremony. R. J. Bauckham points out that Calvin's primary concern with Sabbath ceremonialism is the "manner" of its rigorous observance, which has passed away now that Christ has fulfilled all the typical aspects of the Sabbath.[47] Note Calvin's words to this effect: "However, the ancients did not substitute the Lord's Day (as we call it) for the Sabbath without careful discrimination. The purpose and fulfillment of that true rest, represented by the ancient Sabbath, lies in the Lord's resurrection" (*ICR*, 2.8.34).

In addition, Calvin recognizes that in the fourth commandment there is a moral element that continues, namely that "we must learn to empty ourselves of all our will, of all our thoughts and affections."[48] Sunday observance is intended, as a most pointed example, to call to mind the fact that we are *always* to worship the Lord.[49] In due time, this view was rejected by the Puritans. By the time of the Westminster Assembly, Sabbath keeping had become identified with Puritanism and was, confessionally, an article of faith.

Second, Calvin was not absolutely opposed to the observance of religious days, or holy days. He says, "I shall not condemn churches that have other solemn days for their meetings, provided there be no superstition" (*ICR*, 2.8.34). It is well known that the feasts of Christmas, Easter, Pentecost, and the Ascension were observed in Geneva.[50] In fact, communion observance largely followed the major festivals. "It was administered four times a year: at Easter, at Pentecost, the first Sunday in September, and the Sunday nearest to Christmas."[51] For Calvin, no day was intrinsically more valuable than another, although by the custom of antiquity the Lord's Day was to be highly regarded. Hence, he had no difficulty with the voluntary observance of days that were oriented toward teaching the truths of the gospel. The Puritans, to the contrary, regarded all observance of days—beyond that of the Lord's Day Sabbath—to be in the category of will-worship and therefore unacceptable.[52]

A fourth difference with regard to ceremony is Calvin's view of confirmation. Davies has pointed out that Calvin wished to see the rite of confirmation restored to its proper use in the church.[53] Calvin, speaking of children who had been baptized and grown to years of maturity, recounts his understanding of early church practice. The child was examined by the bishop in reference to his faith. Then, "in order that this act, which ought itself to have been weighty and holy, might have more reverence and dignity, the ceremony of the laying on of hands was also added. . . . Therefore, I warmly approve such laying on of hands, which is simply done as a form of blessing, and wish that it were today restored to pure use" (*ICR*, 4.19.4).

Thomas Becon, chaplain to Thomas Cranmer, provides a similar explanation for the significance of the Anglican ceremony:

> Heretofore we were taught so to bring up our children in the principles of christian religion, that, when they should come to be confirmed of the bishop, they might be able to say the articles of the faith, the Lord's prayer, and the ten commandments, and to answer such questions as are contained in that short catechism, which was appointed to be learned of every child before he were brought to be confirmed.[54]

For the Puritan, there was no biblical basis for confirmation, therefore, no place for it in the worship of the church. William Fulke, for example, complains that confirmation has "displaced catechizing and brought instead thereof vain toys and childish ceremonies to the great hurt of the church."[55] The Westminster Directory contains no provision for confirmation, although the phrase forbidding the "ignorant" to participate, as well as the requirement for "preparatory services," supports the assumption that children were admitted to communion by way of interviews with the session, the method preferred by the Puritans.

Edmund Calamy (grandson of the Westminster divine), writing in justification of the nonconformists expelled in 1662, noted that while some Puritans accepted Anglican confirmation, a number felt it sufficient to "own their Baptismal Covenant understandingly" before the church.[56] The 1661 Exceptions against the Book of Common Prayer makes explicit the Puritan concern that repeating the various formularies of faith was "not sufficient" for admission to communion.[57] Once more, Calvin and the Puritans differ on a specific matter of ceremonial worship.

This leads to the fifth and final area of difference between Calvin and the Puritans. For Calvin, it was quite permissible to use forms of worship that were not divinely commanded. Not only did Calvin use set prayers, but he also used the Apostles' Creed (in a musical version at that!), the *Kyrie Eleison*, and the Lord's Prayer. While not all Puritans were horrified by these particulars, the more consistent among them refused the use of these acts of worship, considering them to be elements that were not commanded in the Scriptures. John Barkley lists "(i) read prayers, (ii) the use of the *Gloria Patri*, (iii) the use of the Creed, (iv) the use of the Lord's Prayer, and (v) kneeling for prayer on entering the pulpit" as falling under the ban.[58] The Westminster Directory at no point authorizes any of these elements, except the Lord's Prayer.

This difference between Calvin and the Puritans is further illustrated by the Puritan practice of limiting church music to the 150 psalms. The Westminster Directory, for example, is quite explicit in its endorsement of exclusive psalmody. Calvin, although favoring psalm-singing, was not a champion of exclusive psalmody. It is an established fact that Calvin's first Psalter included musical versions of the Lord's Prayer, the Decalogue, the Apostles' Creed, and the *Nunc Dimittis*.[59] However this may be explained, it certainly is not compatible with exclusive psalmody. Further, there is evidence that Calvin himself wrote hymns.[60] While it is clear that Calvin had a love for the Psalms, and even favored them above all other church music, he differed with the Puritan position of exclusive psalmody.

CALVIN AND THE CALVINISTS

As we have seen, there are elements of continuity and discontinuity between Calvin and the Puritans. But the question is even more complicated than our discussion has indicated. Davies frames it for us in this way.

> Are the Puritans or the Anglicans to be adjudged the more Reformed in their worship? The answer is that neither is in complete conformity with the Genevan tradition. Whilst the established Church conformed to the mind of Calvin in several matters, such as the pronouncement of Absolution by the Minister, the giving of communion to the sick, the rite of confirmation, the employment of set prayers, the use of a few ceremonies; the Puritans held tenaciously to the accepted customs of the Reformed Churches in such matters as burial, ceremonies, and above all in the exercise of discipline.[61]

For Davies, then, there are clear lines of continuity and discontinuity between Calvin and his two sets of heirs, the Anglicans and the Puritans.

The very possibility that these two groups deviated from Calvin's practice indicates that there must have been some common ground that served as a point of departure. What then was the belief or principle of worship that was common to Calvin, the Anglicans, and the Puritans? J. I. Packer suggests that the common basis the Anglicans and Puritans shared with Calvin was their belief in "the authority and sufficiency of Scripture in all matters of Christian and church life."[62] While there is ample evidence that all parties professed agreement with sentiments similar to this, it is equally clear that much of the controversy in the Church of England revolved around just this affirmation. Packer attempts to explain this phenomenon by arguing that the extended controversy between the Anglicans and the Puritans was over the *application* of this principle, not over the more formal, conceptual question of the authority of Scripture.

Furthermore, the question of application can largely be reduced to one word: *adiaphora.* For the Anglican, the realm of *adiaphora* was broad; for the Puritan, the room given to indifferent matters was severely limited, if not entirely denied.[63] On the positive side, the Puritan hermeneutic did not allow for any area of spiritual life to escape the claims of God's law. On the negative, this was often reduced to a biblicism that sought explicit commands for all of worship. Note, for example, the strictures placed on matters deemed accidental or indifferent by William Ames. "Although there are some 'accidents' or adjuncts in worship, there is no worship which may simply be called accidental, because all worship has in it its own essence. Furthermore, as the least commandments of God even to jots and tittles are to be observed religiously, Matt. 5:18,19, so additions that seem very small are for the same reason rejected."[64]

Ames expressed the same sentiments in his last work, *A Fresh Suit against Human Ceremonies:* "Against the Def. his invention of *indifferent worship,* it was excepted (to passe by repetitions) that no Scripture, Divines, or good reason doeth acknowledge any suche worship. The ground is, because in Scripture, all worship is either approved as good, or condemned as *evill:* all Divines doe distribute worship into *true* or *false:* and they have reson so to doe."[65]

Similar sentiments are evidenced in other Puritan writings

from the same period. John Flavel, for example, echoes the thought of Ames in his own attack on any worship not commanded by God: "And hence it is evident that doctrinal, symbolical ceremonies, I mean such rites and ceremonies as are brought into the worship of God, with a spiritual signification, merely upon the authority of man, are idolatrous mixtures and additions and such by which the Lord is dreadfully provoked."[66] He completes his argument by appealing to a quotation from his fellow Puritan, William Ames. Likewise, John Owen says that "in things which concern the worship of God, the commanding power is Christ, and his command the adequate rule and measure of our obedience."[67]

On the other side of the issue, the Anglican recognized the futility of attempting to justify every particle of worship on the basis of an explicit command. Instead, he was satisfied with a broader, more general conformity to Scripture.[68] This conformity, which removed the most obvious abuses, kept certain traditional practices that were deemed indifferent, but helpful. In the preface to the first Edwardian prayer book, Cranmer wrote that the new book "is more profitable, because here are left out many things, whereof some be untrue, some uncertain, some vain and superstitious: and is ordained nothing to be read, but the very pure word of God, the holy Scriptures, or that which is evidently grounded upon the same."[69] Thus, the Anglican emphasis on things indifferent led to a different understanding of worship, accepting the best in the catholic tradition while seeking a simpler, purer expression of worship.[70]

At this point, it is clear that both parties were unable to hear the truth that the other represented. The Puritan represented that strain in Calvin's thought that demanded biblical warrant and conformity for all of worship, as well as a desire for relative simplicity. The strength of the Puritan theory was its unwavering affirmation of God's sovereign authority over all of life, including worship. The limitation of Puritanism lay in its application of this principle according to overly narrow or minimalist strictures.

The Anglican represented that aspect of Calvin's thought that maintained the necessity of covenantal consciousness, a genuine exercise of dominion and creation within the parameters of what God had revealed. The Anglican further represented Calvin's regard for the ancient church. The failure of Anglicanism and its departure from Calvin lay in its lack of sensitivity for cases of conscience in the imposition of worship. Thus, both Anglicanism and Puritanism represented elements of continuity and discontinuity with Calvin.

THE CRUX INTERPRETUM: COMMANDED OR WARRANTED?

The problem presented here is further elucidated by George Gillespie's discussion of matters indifferent. Gillespie, one of the Scots commissioners to the Westminster Assembly, writes extensively against the Anglican imposition of *adiaphora*, yet provides a sound basis for determining indifferent matters. Gillespie notes a number of significant facts about *adiaphora*. First, there are, ultimately, no *adiaphora*, for men will give an account of every action, thought, or deed.[71] Thus, any discussion of indifferent things must at some point consider the overall context of obedience to the Lord, even as it considers more proximate matters that determine legitimate use. Second, it is impossible to make an absolute distinction between a thing indifferent and the circumstances that surround its use or nonuse.[72] It is not enough to plead the end for which an *adiaphoron* is intended; the circumstances of its use must be considered as well.[73]

Gillespie explains this further. He notes that the circumstances that bear on the proper use of an *adiaphoron* include these issues: (1) Who does it, and does the actor possess proper authority for the action? (2) What is the quality or condition of the object, and is it properly at the disposal of the actor? (3) Where is it done? (4) Is it done lawfully and by proper means? (5) Why is it done (motive)? (6) Is it done with care and unto the Lord? (7) When is it done (e.g., not laboring on the Sabbath)?

Gillespie goes on to elaborate additional rules governing the use of indifferent things. "Every thing which is indifferent in the nature of it, is not by and by indifferent in the use of it. But the use of a thing indifferent ought evermore to be either chosen or re-fused, followed or forsaken, according to these rules delivered to us in God's word: 1. The rule of piety; 2. The rule of charity; 3. The rule of purity."[74] As Gillespie explains, the rule of piety means that all actions must be done as unto the Lord. The rule of charity means that the use of indifferent things must consider their effect on the church. The rule of purity demands that all be done with a clean conscience before God and without doubt. He summarizes, "Since a thing indifferent in the nature of it can never be lawfully used, except according to these rules, hence it followeth, that the use of a thing indifferent is never lawful to us when we have no other warrant for using the same beside our own will and arbitrement."[75]

In these words, Gillespie has expressed a view of *adiaphora* and the regulation of worship that differs little, if at all, from the views expressed by John Calvin. The question, however, does not lie in the realm of the conceptual. Rather, the question is more appropriately over the nature of *adiaphora* and whether it is legitimate to apply this concept of "indifference" broadly to circumstances of worship. It is interesting to note that while rightly insisting on commands for elements of worship, and providing a basis for *adiaphora*, Gillespie's application of *adiaphora* is, in practice, greatly constricted. In their theology of worship Gillespie and the Puritans failed to maintain a broad application of *adiaphora* to circumstances.

To elaborate further, there is no doubt that John Calvin professed adherence to the principle that worship should be regulated. However, it is evident that his application of that principle differed significantly from that of his disciples, especially the English Puritans. More importantly, the application of that principle differed because the formulation of that principle differed. That is, although it has been established that Calvin sought conformity to the Word of God in matters of worship, the more radical Puritans differed from Calvin in two specific ways.

First, they interpreted the regulative principle far more rigorously than did Calvin. "It can be shown that the Puritans who wanted 'a reformation without tarrying for any' were more scrupulous in carrying out Calvin's doctrines to their logical conclusion than the logical Reformer himself. While Calvin, as his biographer Doumergue has shewn, admitted a 'principle of accommodation' in inessential matters, his English disciples admitted of no compromise."[76] For Calvin, then, the requirement could be described quite simply as "whatever is consistent with the Scripture." That is not the same as the Puritan "whatever is commanded by Scripture."

Second, the Puritan application of the regulative principle differed from Calvin in its more rigorous requirements for circumstances and its restrictive understanding of *adiaphora*. The Puritan position is related to Calvin's position, but as an exaggeration, a more extreme rule that does not achieve the full biblical balance and catholicity of Calvin's position. As James Jordan has described the situation, "The Reformers had realized that God's 'commands' are found in Scripture in 'precept, principle, and example.' Their heirs tended to exchange this holistic openness to the Word of God for a quest for 'explicit commands.' "[77]

The contrast is now quite clear. The Puritan formula could be reduced to the simple disjunction: "either commanded (or a necessary logical consequence of such a command) or unlawful." This is more than Calvin required, and it demonstrates a significant deviation from the principles of Calvin's reform. But the larger question still remains unanswered. What does the Scripture itself require? It is to that question that we must now turn our attention.

Chapter 6

THY WILL BE DONE

*I*n considering the biblical evidence advanced for the regulative principle, it is first necessary to admit that there is a tremendous amount of material that could be deemed appropriate. Indeed there is a thorough compilation of relevant texts and exegetical discussions in the Reformed Presbyterian Church of North America's volume *The Biblical Doctrine of Worship*. It almost goes without saying that such a considerable amount of textual material is far beyond the scope of this work. And a number of the texts in question are not particularly relevant to the immediate question.[1] This does not mean that they are unimportant. Rather, the point is that the majority of the traditional interpretations of the prooftexts for the regulative principle of worship are sound, in so far as strict exegesis itself is concerned. The question that remains, however, is, How do we understand these texts in light of the worship practices of our Lord?

Our challenge, then, lies in the following two areas: (1) understanding the nature of Puritan biblical interpretation, and (2) integrating the practices of Jesus concerning the worship of God into our understanding of the regulation of worship. These will be discussed to determine whether the biblical data do require the strict Puritan formulation of the regulative principle. In the course of these discussions, we will consider citations from selected writings that represent the fully matured Puritan position as codified at the Westminster Assembly.

PURITAN THOUGHT AND BIBLICAL INTERPRETATION

In properly evaluating the Puritan regulative principle of worship, one compelling fact remains: the Puritans considered themselves biblical in their theology and in their exegesis. That is, their allegiance above all was to the authority of Scripture as God's Word.[2] However, the Puritans' commitment to the absolute authority of the Scriptures does not protect them from errors of interpretation or methodology or make them immune to the historical limitations of their time. While the errors of the Puritans were relatively minor, and their contributions to biblical and theological studies immense, the fact remains that certain peculiarities and limitations of the period were conducive to establishing their particular formulation of the regulative principle of worship.

Puritanism was not a static position. Instead, under continual pressure from the established church, Puritanism steadily embraced increasingly radical positions. As these positions hardened, the Puritan regulative principle of worship was applied in a new and more rigorous way. The Puritans' errors in interpretation, theology, and practice do not vitiate the principle that worship should be regulated. They do, however, call into question the particular form they gave to that principle. Extremism always involves imbalance, and the Puritan regulative principle of worship was imbalanced in a number of ways. These will be considered briefly in the following survey.

SIMPLE, SPIRITUAL WORSHIP

The first area in which the Puritan regulative principle of worship went astray is demonstrated in, and highlighted by, the Puritan tendency toward rationalism. "Briefly, the puritan theory is that worship is a purely *mental* activity, to be exercised by a strictly psychological 'attention' to a subjective emotional or spiritual experience."[3] The problem here addressed is described by the philosophical and psychological concept often labeled the "primacy of the intellect." This position argues for the necessary primacy of reason and intellect in the pursuit of truth. Cornelius Van Til, however, has demonstrated the pagan origin of this concept and has argued, instead, that the primacy of the intellect should be viewed as an unfortunate consequence of the fall into sin.[4] Thus, Van Til would argue that the will, the emotions, and the intellect all have value before God, are redeemed in Christ, and have the capacity to please God equally in their wise use and development.[5] To their detriment, many Puritans were influenced by the prevailing tendencies of their age, tendencies exhibited in the Cartesian shift from objective truth to personal truth, from the primacy of revelation to the primacy of reason. This intellectual environment was conducive to the intellectualizing of worship.

For the Puritan, appeal to the senses or emotions through ceremony and rite was but an appeal to man's carnal nature. One author has contrasted the tendencies of the "catholic" spirit and the Puritan. "The type of mind called 'catholic' is apt to build up a too elaborate system of rites, ceremonies, and ordinances, and thus to confuse the material with the spiritual. On the other hand, the Puritan is apt to place too much importance upon the reason and the intellect, and, in consequence, is in danger of becoming dogmatic and hard."[6] Similarly, John New, while speaking of the Puritan "fixation upon the Word," notes that the biblical emphasis of Puritanism often obscured an underlying rationalistic bent.[7]

This rationalistic bent did not rule out other motives in Puritan religious sentiment. The presence of religious enthusiasm as well as mystical tendencies has been well documented.[8] In working out this bent, the Puritan often equated spiritual worship, or simple worship, with that which speaks to the heart through the mind. Geoffrey F. Nuttall notes "simplicity," in general, to be one of the hallmarks of Puritanism.[9] To involve the body in worship, to do anything other than engage in simple, spiritual worship, was considered an act of idolatry. George Gillespie, for example, is clear in this regard: "The policy, then, which is most simple and single, and least lustred with the pomp and bravery of ceremonies, cannot but be most expedient for edification."[10] He goes on further to contrast external worship with spiritual worship and concludes that the Anglican ceremonies should be condemned "because they derogate from the true inward and spiritual worship."[11]

Gillespie was not alone in these sentiments. Note these words from John Flavel, another Puritan authority:

> Now, hence you may come to see at once, both the nature of this second sort of idolatry, and also the rise and original of it; which is nothing else but the proud and carnal heart of man, which not willing to contain itself within the limits of the word, wherein a plain, simple, and spiritual way of worship is ruled out, invents to itself new rites, ceremonies, and ways of worshipping God.[12]

Likewise, John Owen argues for gospel simplicity:

> "God is a Spirit, and will be worshipped in spirit and in truth," John iv.24. And no devotion is acceptable unto him, but what proceedeth from and is an effect of faith. . . . These things [i.e., religious rites and ceremonies not commanded in Scripture], herefore, being utterly destitute of

divine authority, they can no way further or promote the devotion of the worshippers. What natural or carnal affections may be excited by them,—as men may "inflame themselves with idols," Isa. lvii.5,—or what outward, outside devotion they may direct unto or excite, is uncertain; but that they are no means of stirring up the grace of God in the hearts of believers, or of the increase or strengthening of their faith,—which things alone God accepts in gospel worship,—seeing they are not appointed by him for any such purpose, is most certain.[13]

Of course, both Flavel and Owen exhibit abundant evidence of warmth and piety in their writings and their lives; but the tendency to rationalism remains a fixture in *their thinking*.

How can this be explained? Some have attempted to ascribe the rationalistic bent, and the ascetic spirit that often accompanied Puritan religion, to neo-Platonic influences[14] or to "western stoic philosophy."[15] The Puritans were decidedly not antimaterialistic in their approach to life in general. They were not affected by an underlying Manichaeism. However, their fear of idolatry and their polemic with, first, the Roman Catholics and, second, the Anglicans did lead them to an imbalance in matters of worship. It is true that Stoicism made inroads into late–sixteenth-century thought in general and seventeenth-century Puritanism in particular.[16] Further, it is also true that neo-Platonic influences arrived officially on the Puritan academic horizon by the mid–seventeenth century with the rise of the Cambridge Platonists (and had been influencing European humanist thought from the time of Marsilio Ficino).[17] In view of the fact that elements of Stoicism and neo-Platonism were part of the intellectual milieu of the period, it is reasonable to conclude that these systems, running in parallel with the Puritans' own ascetic leanings, exerted some influence on their thinking.

Errors in Hermeneutics

The second area in which the Puritan regulative principle of worship suffers defects is demonstrated by some peculiarities in their interpretation of Scripture. That is, there were a number of errors in the hermeneutical methods employed by the Puritans. One of these defects is the crass literalism present in the application of the regulative principle. J. I. Packer has summarized some of the more notable of the errors resulting from this literalism. He notes that these extreme examples, not representative of Puritanism in general, were the results of consistent application of the principle that all worship "must have direct biblical warrant."

> The attempt to put the Puritan ideal of church life and worship on to this footing led to some curiosities of argument, such as the "proof" that catechising was a duty, from "hold fast the form of sound words" (2 Tim. i:13); or the "proof" that liturgical forms were unlawful, from Romans viii:26; or the "proof" that the minister should stand in one place throughout the service from "Peter stood up in the midst of the disciples" (Acts i:15); or the "proof" of the necessity of the controversial "prophesyings" (area preaching meetings, at which several ministers spoke successively on the same passage of Scripture), from I Corinthians xiv:31 ("ye may all prophesy one by one, that all may learn and all may be comforted").[18]

These somewhat humorous interpretations occur as a result of an erroneous assumption about biblical teaching. As James Jordan explains, "The fact is, the Bible teaches by implication as well as by direct statement. A preoccupation with a strict, literal basis for worship is not a principle of interpretation consistent with the Bible itself."[19]

Another defect in the Puritan interpretation of Scripture is, at times, an atomistic handling of individual texts. The exegesis of individual texts is absolutely necessary for doing theology. Furthermore, even the use of prooftexts per se, should not be disparaged if those texts are handled properly. Exegetical errors, however, contributed to the Puritan formulation of the regulative principle of worship. For example, it is possible to isolate texts for a particular doctrine or proposition, and then to interpret them in such a way that they do not provide for systemic unity. To handle individual texts in an *ad hoc, ad seriatim* fashion may fail to synthesize accurately the overall message of the Scriptures. In other words, there is a failure to consider the analogy of faith.[20]

This does not mean that the Puritans in general, or the Westminster divines in particular, were not systematic. Indeed, their legacy is one of thorough, consistent Reformed constructs in theology. Rather, the point is that some Puritans, when interpreting a text that had bearing on the regulative principle of worship, failed to take into account the larger context of the Scriptures. As a case in point, the frequent Puritan usage of passages forbidding any "adding to" what God has commanded usually ignores the relevance of intertestamental and New Testament Jewish practice. The result is a synthesis of Scripture that is only partial.

Likewise, individual texts are often maximized by logical extension, so that too much weight is given to "necessary consequences."[21] The use of logic and necessary consequence in doing theology is not only a tool of Puritans but, commonly, of all theologians; and, when balanced with the overall teaching of Scripture, this is not necessarily a problem. However, when a text is isolated and stretched beyond the clear, exegetical import, the necessary consequence or logical conclusion may be more a case of reading into the text than reading out of the text.[22] No doubt some of the minutiae pertaining to questions of polity and worship were less "necessary " than the Puritans often portrayed them to be. For example, George Gillespie argues that since there is no explicit mention of worship in Esther 9:19, 22, there was no religious significance to Purim. This is hardly a necessary consequence and seems far wide of the mark.[23]

The overemphasis on logic leads, naturally, to another possible error in interpretation. Often Puritan exegesis failed to take into account organic biblical developments. That is, the redemptive-historical character of revelation is, at times, neglected. For example, any discussion of Mosaic regulation of worship should also consider Davidic contributions to worship, exilic and postexilic developments, and relevant data from the New Testament, including dominical and apostolic teaching and practice. Biblical theology, of course, is a relatively new discipline; so to accuse the Puritans of errors in biblical theology would be anachronistic. Nonetheless, there are certain basic principles in doing theology that any interpreter of Scripture—in any age—must adhere to, whether formally or informally. One of these is the necessity of placing textual material in a true historical context.[24] This demands not only an understanding of the cultural setting of the text, but also an awareness of the text in light of the progressive unfolding of redemption.

Unfortunately, there are errors in the way in which the Puritan interpreters handled these matters. For example, in dealing with the definition of worship, the Westminster Confession of Faith, 21.1, uses prooftexts that had relevance in a particular cultural setting, namely the entrance of Israel into a land in which paganism was the dominant religious system: Joshua 24:14; Deuteronomy 4:15–20; 12:32; Exodus 20:4–6, among others. Certainly these texts would be a part of an overall theology of worship, but to absolutize them without due regard for their cultural setting is to distort their place in a developed theology of worship and their relevance for contemporary challenges.[25] This is simply a failure to distinguish between the strict exegesis of a passage and the interpretation and application of the passage.

A corollary to this failure to grasp the organic development of the Scriptures is the failure to relate properly the New Testament to the Old Testament. In too many situations, the Puritan attitude toward the Old Testament became one of disparagement. The Old Testament, for many, did not provide normative guidelines for worship, but was completely superseded by the New Testament.[26] Note, for example, these words of John Owen in which he argues against the validity of Christians praying the Lord's Prayer:

> Our Savior at that time was minister of the Circumcision, and taught the doctrine of the gospel under and with the observation of all the worship of the Judaical church. He was not yet glorified, and so the Spirit was not as yet given; I mean that Spirit which he promised unto his disciples to enable them to perform all the worship of God by him required at their hands, whereof we have before spoken. That, then, which the Lord Jesus prescribed unto his disciples, for their present practice in the worship of God, seems to have belonged unto the economy of the Old Testament. Now to argue from the prescription of, and outward helps for, the performance of the worship of God under the Old Testament, unto a necessity of the like or the same under the New, is upon the matter to deny that Christ is ascended on high, and to have given spiritual gifts unto men eminently distinct from and above those given out by him under the Judaical pedagogy.[27]

Here, in addition to his odd notion regarding the Lord's Prayer, Owen seems to have adopted a hermeneutic that places the Old Testament on a lower level than the New Testament, at least in matters of worship. This is seen later in the same work where he says, "In things which concern the worship of God, the commanding power is Christ, and his command the adequate rule and measure of our obedience."[28] This preoccupation with the New Testament is a standard Puritan point of emphasis[29] and undermines a biblical basis for worship that includes Old Testament data as normative as well.[30] Indeed, one of the greatest of all ironies is the noninstrumental, psalm-singing Presbyterian who sings Psalm 150 acappella![31]

In conclusion, it must be said that not all Puritans were guilty of committing all of these errors. Further, even the commission of a number of these errors was not sufficient to undermine their theological endeavors totally. They were all far too much men of the Word to stray significantly. Nevertheless, the cumulative effect of these errors was to exaggerate the requirements of Scripture in reference to the regulation of worship and to contribute to the formulation of the Puritan regulative principle of worship.

DOMINICAL PRACTICES AND THE REGULATIVE PRINCIPLE

Of particular significance for the formulation of a regulating principle of worship are those texts that set forth the worship practices of our Lord. Undoubtedly, a complete study of the teachings and practices of Jesus Christ regarding worship would be of enormous value. In fact, John Murray has observed that one brief utterance of Jesus on the nature of worship, John 4:24, is alone worth a complete dissertation.[32] Granting the truth of Murray's observation, it is immediately apparent that the intent of this section must be limited in scope. Therefore, we will pursue only one very pointed question. That is, What do the worship practices of our Lord teach us about the proper regulation of worship?

Of course, much of the discussion concerning the worship practices of Jesus would involve his keeping the Old Testament law in its integrity. About this there is no significant controversy. Jesus is quite zealous in maintaining the integrity of both the inward attitude and the outward observance.[33] Clearly, in John 4:24, he teaches that true worship must link together the inward and outward and must exhibit the characteristics of truthfulness and spirituality. Concerning John 4:24, C. K. Barrett notes:

It follows that Christian worship is *en pneumati* [in spirit], just as it is *en aletheia* [in truth], and it is impossible to separate the two notions (note that neither in v. 24 nor in v. 23 is *en* repeated before *aletheia*). *en pneumati* draws attention to the supernatural life that Christians enjoy, and *en aletheia* to the single basis of this supernatural life in Christ through whom God's will is faithfully fulfilled.[34]

This emphasis is highlighted by the contrast that Jesus so often makes between the commandments of men and the commandments of God, as in Matthew 15:2–9 and Mark 7:1–13, the controversy over washing, or in Luke 6:1–10, the controversy over Sabbath observance. Murray summarizes the significance of this pervasive emphasis in Jesus' teaching:

The repeated reference to the commandment of God is of paramount importance. It shows that nothing less than this is in our Lord's esteem the regulative principle of the worship of God. It does not mean that "tradition" as such is to be depreciated. *But it does require that any tradition which is not based upon and derived from divine prescription is of human origin and sanction and incurs the condemnation so patent in our Lord's teaching on this subject.* Jesus' cleansing of the temple illustrates his jealousy for the sanctity of the house of God and the holy zeal with which desecration should be expelled.[35]

Murray's summary has two points in its favor: (1) it has the strength of agreeing with the Puritan tradition, and (2) it does appear to be a reasonable inference from the passages considered. But can Murray's summary stand the scrutiny of additional New Testament data? Is it possible that another interpretation may be found that is a legitimate understanding of the texts at hand? These are the questions that now must be addressed.

The Synagogue

One issue that is casually skirted by proponents of the traditional view is the question of synagogue worship. According to the Puritan regulative principle, only that which is directly commanded by God or may be concluded by due and necessary inference is a legitimate element of worship. Is synagogue worship compatible with the above definition? On the one hand, the facts would indicate that the synagogue, if viewed as an element of worship, is incompatible with the Puritan formulation and would fall into the category the Puritans described as will-worship. On the other hand, if viewed as a circumstance of worship, the synagogue would fit well with Calvin's broad understanding of *adiaphora*, but not so well with Puritanism's restricted understanding of circumstances. The following discussion will focus on three issues: (1) the origin of the synagogue, (2) the worship of the synagogue, and (3) the practice of Jesus relative to the synagogue.

To begin with, the origin of the synagogue appears to be of human contrivance and not of divine command. "The origin of the house of prayer, later known as the synagogue, is recorded neither in the Bible nor in the post-biblical records. Only scattered hints can be discovered in the vast rabbinic literature. But these vague hints enable us to make some plausible conjectures. The most logical of these is that the synagogue had its origin in spontaneous informal gatherings among the Jewish exiles in Babylonia."[36] It must be granted, however, that there is not a complete unanimity of thinking on the origin of the synagogue. Rabbinical tradition locates the origin during the time of Moses. More recently, James Jordan has found the origin of the synagogue in Leviticus 23:3 and thus considers it a Mosaic institution. In fact, Jordan sees the synagogue functioning as a protolocal church within the national church, Israel.[37] However, his proposal, undermined by his own admission that "we have little information" about the pre-exilic synagogue, is not widely received by scholars.[38]

By contrast, the available evidence is overwhelmingly in favor of an exilic or postexilic origin. Notably, the destruction of the temple, which is the very reason for the development of the synagogue, occurred centuries after the time of Moses. Indeed, "the pattern of weekly worship did not exist in the Old Testament law."[39] Again, the evidence is overwhelming that the synagogue developed late in Jewish history as a human response to the end of temple worship.[40] Moreover, there is no evidence of a specific divine command to establish such an institution, nor to develop a liturgy according to the synagogue pattern. Douglas Bannerman, however, does see in the gradual development of synagogue worship the providential hand of God at work, preparing for the transition from Old Testament temple worship to the New Testament *ecclesia*.[41]

The synagogue, of course, was a problem for the Puritans and their strict construction of the regulative principle of worship.[42] George Gillespie, familiar with all the previous arguments and writing with the express intent of removing this obstacle to the Puritan view, addressed the origin of the synagogue in his *A Dispute against the English Popish Ceremonies*. Gillespie's argument was basically twofold. First, he asserted the view that synagogue worship was a very ancient and necessary institution. "After the tribes were settled in the land of promise, synagogues were built, in the case of an urgent necessity, because all Israel could not come every Sabbath day to the reading and expounding of the law in the place which God had chosen that his name might dwell there."[43]

This part of Gillespie's argument fails, not only because of the proof for the late development of the synagogue, but also in view of the fact that there is no evidence for any authorized Old Testament worship other than personal, familial, or public worship in relation to the tabernacle or temple.[44]

The second argument is a curious one in which Gillespie shifts the burden of proof to his opponents, demanding that they prove his rather bizarre assertion to be incorrect: "If Formalists will make any advantage of the building of synagogues, they must prove that they were founded, not upon the extraordinary warrant of prophets, but upon that ordinary power which the church retaineth still."[45] This argument from silence begs the question and requires no refutation. It does, however, warrant comment. It is clear that Gillespie recognized the importance this argument had for his view of the regulation of worship. Otherwise it is doubtful he would have devised a defense so unusual and so desperate. Gillespie, operating out of a constricted view of *adiaphora*, could not envision the synagogue as circumstantial. His narrow understanding of circumstances forced him to view it as elemental or essential and, consequently, to provide some justification, however tenuous, for its divine origin.

This leads, naturally enough, to consideration of the worship or liturgy of the synagogue. As noted, the synagogue originally developed in the vacuum created by the destruction of the temple and the exile. Hence the nature of synagogue worship differed from temple worship in that the priestly and sacrificial elements as prescribed in the law were never a part of synagogue worship. There was no usurping of temple prerogatives. Rather, temple and synagogue "coexisted harmoniously."[46]

However, there were acts of worship, not constitutive of temple worship, that became customary and were institutionalized during the intertestamental era.[47] The order of synagogue worship, as practiced in the New Testament era, would have appeared as follows: (1) the antiphonal recitation of the *shema*; (2) liturgical prayers—the "eighteen benedictions" (or, on the Sabbath, seven benedictions) and responses; and (3) the reading of the Torah and Haftorah[48] with the ceremonial kissing of the scroll and liturgical responses by the congregation, followed by an exhortation or exposition based upon the readings.[49]

The significance of this portrayal for the issue at hand is clear. While thoroughly consistent with Old Testament faith and practice, the structure, the responses, and even the very existence of the liturgy itself all lack explicit biblical command. Thus, the normal liturgy of the synagogue was largely of human origin and included ceremony (actions) and ritual (words or texts) clearly not of divine origin. This is highlighted by James Charlesworth's assertion that "many hymns and prayers that were eventually not included in the Jewish or Christian canons were often used authoritatively in Jewish services prior to, and during, the time of Jesus."[50] Further, the liturgy, with its accompanying rites and ceremonies, constituted the worship in which Jesus participated. The importance of these facts for the regulation of worship—and the definition of circumstances—cannot be overstated.

Finally, we turn to the third consideration, namely, the practice of Jesus relative to the synagogue. The first recorded visit of Jesus to a synagogue is found in Luke 4:16–30. The key consideration in the passage, the statement that relates to this investigation, is Luke's assertion in verse 16. Speaking of Jesus, Luke says, "On the Sabbath day he went into the synagogue, as was his custom." That is, Jesus regularly attended the synagogue to worship the Lord. Joseph Fitzmyer summarizes the significance of this verse: "Luke alone among the Synoptic evangelists stresses Jesus' habitual frequenting of the synagogue; he thus presents him conforming to the general Jewish custom described by Josephus (*Ant.* 16.2,4 &43) of giving 'every seventh day over to the study of our customs and laws.' "[51] Fitzmyer here emphasizes the fact that Jesus made a practice of attendance at the synagogue. Further, he points to the additional salient feature of this passage, namely, that Jesus worshiped at the synagogue in accordance with the usual practice of any other adult Jewish male.[52]

Gary Cohen summarizes the evidence concerning Jesus' relation to the synagogue throughout his ministry: "Thus it is observed that Christ habitually taught on the Sabbath in the synagogue of the region that He was ministering in at the time. During these visitations He cast out demons, healed, and revealed Himself."[53] Jesus, then, frequented a place of worship established without divine command, the synagogue. Further, he worshiped in the synagogue according to Jewish practice and followed liturgical forms, ceremonies, and rites that were of human origin. *Jesus, in his practice, violated the Puritan formulation of the regulative principle of worship.* This does not undermine the principle that God regulates worship. It does mean, however, that the Puritan formulation is faulty and must be reconsidered in light of the practice of Jesus himself.

VOLUNTARY JEWISH FEASTS

In the Old Testament, various festivals were instituted as required elements of Jewish worship. The most important of these were the *"festival pilgrimages,* when the whole congregation assembled at the sanctuary."[54] These feasts were (1) Passover, (2) the Feast of Weeks, or Pentecost, and (3) the Feast of Tabernacles and the Day of Atonement. The key importance of these feasts lies in the fact that their observance was a matter of divine imperative, and their proper observation was the subject of detailed prescription.

There is no question that Jesus observed these Jewish feasts.[55] However, there is also clear evidence that Jesus observed at least one, and possibly two Jewish feasts that are not of Mosaic origin. More important, the Jewish festivals that are post-Mosaic are clearly of human origin and not divine. The first example is found in John 10:22: "Then came the Feast of Dedication at Jerusalem." The history of this particular feast is most relevant to the present discussion. Alfred Edersheim describes it as follows:

> It was not of Biblical origin, but had been instituted by Judas Maccabeus in 164 B.C., when the Temple, which had been desecrated by Antiochus Epiphanes, was once more purified, and rededicated to the Service of Jehovah. Accordingly, it was designated as "the Dedication of the Altar." Josephus calls it "The Lights." . . . The Jews called it

Chanukkah, "dedication" or "consecration," and, in much the same sense, *Enkainia* in the Greek of the LXX, and in the New Testament.[56]

A superficial reading of the passage would imply that Jesus was present for the purpose of observing the feast[57] even when there was no particular messianic purpose cited for that visit.[58]

Samuel Andrews attributes Jesus' presence in Jerusalem to "some special motive," but assumes he would have observed the festival wherever he was.[59] Gillespie, recognizing the importance of this event, argues the following points: (1) that there was no legal basis for the Feast of Dedication, (2) that Christ did not approve of the feast, and (3) that his presence was entirely for the benefit of the multitude, not due to any regard he may have had for the festival.[60] Consider the facts, however. At what other time in the ministry of Jesus did he accommodate himself to the religious errors of the Jews, for whatever reason? The desperation in Gillespie's efforts to reconcile this event with the Puritan regulative principle of worship should be obvious.

Significantly, the commentators disagree with Gillespie's speculation. There is virtual unanimity among the commentators that Jesus was there *to worship*. Calvin, for example, notes that "Christ appeared *in the temple* at that time, according to custom." He further understands this passage as displaying Jesus' conformity to the religious practice of the Jews.[61] Leon Morris says, "Jesus followed the practice of the pious men of His day by going up to Jerusalem to observe festivals."[62] From a redaction-critical perspective, Raymond Brown assumes that Jesus was present for the observation of the festival. He notes that the material is "traditional" and rejects the idea "that the saying would have been responsible for the setting."[63]

There is further evidence that Jesus' presence at the festival indicated his approval of this particular religious observance. One of the tasks of Jesus' messianic ministry was that of fulfilling the law. (See Matthew 5:17b, "I have not come to abolish . . . but to fulfill.") On this passage, John Murray, a proponent of the Puritan regulative principle of worship, comments, "He came to realize the full measure of the intent and purpose of the law and the prophets. He came to complete, to consummate, to bring to full fruition and perfect fulfillment the law and the prophets."[64] While it is true that fulfillment of the divinely instituted law was mandated, it is pertinent to note that Jesus also is the God-sent fulfillment of this humanly instituted Festival of Dedication, or Lights. Leon Morris notes two particular lines of fulfillment in this passage. He observes that John perhaps has in mind the ensuing dedication of Jesus as the true temple of God as well as the related thought that Jesus is the true light that brings men out of darkness.[65] Both of these concepts relate to the major themes of this feast.

B. F. Westcott comments that "the special mention of the time ['Then came the Feast of Dedication'] appears to be made in order to connect the subject of the Lord's teaching with the hopes associated with the last national deliverance."[66] More evidence supporting the idea of fulfillment is provided by Barrett and Brown, who also find thematic connections between the feast (and its significance) and Jesus' teaching concerning himself (John 10:22–39).[67] To summarize this evidence, Jesus attends the Feast of Dedication (Lights) and uses the occasion to point out that he himself is the fulfillment of the two major themes celebrated in this feast. While this is not in the same category as the observance of Passover (which was divinely mandated and therefore required its antitypical fulfillment), Jesus' use of the feast as an occasion to show himself as its true fulfillment nonetheless demonstrates the high value he placed upon this voluntary feast, a feast clearly ascribed to human origin and not divine command.

A further consideration, although of relatively less weight, is Jesus' observance of the festival of John 5:1: "Some time later, Jesus went up to Jerusalem for a feast of the Jews." The discussions over the identification of this feast have been extensive, the evidence minimal, and the conclusions uncertain. Nevertheless, it should be noted that among the conclusions, "most commentators favor Purim or Passover."[68] Of course, there is no way of attaining certainty on this matter, so it is best not to be overly assertive. However, the textual evidence does argue strongly against the inclusion of the definite article before "feast," and this at least points away from one of the major pilgrim feasts.[69] If the suggestion of Purim (which celebrates the deliverance of the Jews under Esther from the wicked plan of Haman to exterminate them) is correct, this would explain why the article is absent and the feast, as a lesser observance, is unnamed.

Most important, if this is a reference to Purim, another example is provided in which Jesus attends a festival of religious import with its own liturgical observance—a festival not instituted by divine command. Of course, apart from the question of Jesus' attendance, the very existence of Purim among the Jews (purged from their sin of idolatry) and its establishment in the Book of Esther by the Jews are significant for this discussion. Consider these words from Esther 9:18–28:

> The Jews in Susa, however, had assembled on the thirteenth and fourteenth, and then on the fifteenth they rested and made it a day of feasting and joy. . . .
>
> Mordecai recorded these events, and he sent letters to all the Jews throughout the provinces of King Xerxes, near and far, to have them celebrate annually the fourteenth and fifteenth days of the month of Adar as the time when the Jews got relief from their enemies, and as the month when their sorrow was turned into joy and their mourning into a day of celebration. He wrote them to observe the days as days of feasting and joy and giving presents of food to one another and gifts to the poor.
>
> So the Jews agreed to continue the celebration they had begun, doing what Mordecai had written to them. [Therefore these days were called Purim, from the word *pur*.] . . .

Because of everything written in this letter and because of what they had seen and what had happened to them, *the Jews took it upon themselves to establish the custom that they and their descendants and all who join them should without fail observe these two days every year,* in the way prescribed and at the time appointed. These days should be remembered and observed in every generation by every family, and in every province and in every city. And these days of Purim should never cease to be celebrated by the Jews, nor should the memory of them die out among their descendants. [emphasis added]

The establishment of Purim is problematic enough for the Puritan regulative principle of worship, even apart from the participation of Jesus. It is most significant that while Jesus reproves the Jews for many breaches of the covenant, he never expresses condemnation of the voluntary feasts of Dedication and Purim. Instead, he was there with the Jews, sanctifying these practices by his presence.

The evidence concerning the worship practices of our Lord has significantly undermined the traditional Puritan formulation of the regulative principle of worship. Indeed, the Puritan principle fails to account for the synagogue and the post-Mosaic festivals. For the Puritan, they are elements of worship and therefore must be justified by the principle or explained away! The forced exegesis and arguments from silence demonstrate the inadequacy of the Puritan formula.

Moreover, under the Puritan regulative principle of worship, it is impossible to explain the actions of our Lord! Yet the synagogue and festivals do not constitute new elements of worship. Rather, they are focused and intentional *circumstances* of worship that flow out of the religious life of God's covenant people. As such, they find no place in the Puritan regulative principle of worship, although they do find a place in the dominical practice of worship! With new insight into our Lord's practice of worship, we turn our attention now to the relationship between life and worship.

Chapter 7

YOUR REASONABLE SERVICE

*A*ll that has preceded has been helpful in determining that the regulative principle of worship, as formulated by the Puritans, adopted by the Westminster Assembly, and embraced by the various Presbyterian churches, is flawed and unworkable. More important, it does not reflect accurately the practice of our Lord himself. Does this mean, then, that worship is a matter of complete freedom, subject to individual tastes or corporate ecclesiastical dictates?

On the contrary, the fact that the Puritan regulative principle of worship has been found wanting does not mean that the Scriptures fail to give guidance concerning the regulation of worship. In fact, the Puritans were on the right track in their insistence that worship is to be determined by the Word of God. The Bible does provide direction for acceptable worship. It does give information for the people of God to use in evaluating forms of worship. Clearly there are elements of worship that are commanded and governed by precepts. And clearly there are circumstances of worship that are governed by a far less rigorous set of principles.

Life in covenant with God is not conducted with reference to an endless series of rules designed for every conceivable occasion. And as we shall see, that is not the way the worship of God should be conducted either. Therefore, our thoughts now will be directed toward establishing the covenant context of worship. Three key ideas will be examined. First, we will consider the biblical and theological principles that relate all of life to worship. Second, we will consider the rehabilitation of *adiaphora* based on selected New Testament texts. Third, we will examine the confessional tradition of the Reformed churches to determine their teaching on *adiaphora*. These concepts, separate but related, will direct us toward a firm foundation for the regulation of worship.

LIFE AS WORSHIP

The biblical and theological considerations that have preceded have provided a foundation for further consideration. At this point in the discussion, a new key idea must be introduced. Simply put, we must reexamine the traditional understanding of worship. By confining worship to a corporate, public event, it is possible, at best, to arrive at only a very narrow definition of worship. However, in recent literature it has become conventional to speak of all of life as worship. That is, the Christian life itself is considered to be worship, and *the corporate, public event is seen as a point of concentration.* Paul Hoon, for example, has rejected the idea that worship is circumscribed by cult and has provided direction toward viewing life as worship. "Very simply, our traditional understanding of worship as restricted to the cultic gathering of the congregation at a designated time and place for rite and proclamation will no longer do. This is not what the New Testament means by worship. Rather, worship in New Testament terms is a comprehensive category describing the Christian's total existence, and it is to be thought of as coextensive with man's faith-response wherever and whenever this response occurs."[1]

This same concept has been discussed at length by Robert Morey in his *Worship Is All of Life* and by John MacArthur in *The Ultimate Priority*. In his volume, Morey defines worship as consisting of several ascending stages. Beginning with the broadest application of worship as "all of life," Morey concentrates his focus on each successive step. He adds to worship as life the individual's private worship before God, family worship, and, finally, corporate public worship. Central to his thesis is the priority of worship as a mode of living. Referring to the 24th Psalm, he notes, "The psalmist believed that every square inch of this universe and all of life belong to God. There is no neutral or secular area of life. Every act of obedience to God in thought, word or deed is worship."[2] This, then, is the basis for all aspects of worship, whether conducted privately and individually, in families, or as corporate, public acts of the believing congregation.[3]

John MacArthur's emphasis is similar. He criticizes what he perceives to be the misplaced emphasis that has dominated past discussions on worship:

> So-called worship seems little more than some liturgy (high or low) equated with stained-glass windows, organ music, or emotion-filled songs and prayers. If the bulletin didn't say "Worship Service," maybe we wouldn't know what we were supposed to be doing. And that reflects the absence of a worshiping life — of which a Sunday service is to be only a corporate overflow.[4]

For MacArthur, then, only after one has established life as worship can one truly discuss focused or concentrated points of worship such as the public assembly on the Lord's Day.

RELATION OF LIFE TO WORSHIP

While Hoon, Morey, and MacArthur are clearly sympathetic, to some degree, with rethinking the nature of worship, the idea that all of life is worship is present in the writings of one who is firmly committed to the historic Puritan regulative principle of worship. In his treatment of the regulative principle, Norman Shepherd broadens the discussion to what he describes as the regulative principle for life.[5] Shepherd describes this principle as follows: "Our way of acceptability to God and the maintenance of communion with God is wholly and exclusively determined by God in his law to which nothing may be added and from which nothing may be subtracted."[6] Thus for Shepherd, it is possible to speak of things as *adiaphora* in a proximate sense only, while "in the ultimate sense, there are no *adiaphora*."[7]

The importance of this concept for the Puritan regulative principle may be demonstrated easily. "The regulative principle for worship is simply a specific, indeed the most pointed application of the regulative principle for life because worship is at the heart of our communion with God."[8] Of course, Shepherd's intent is to establish the Puritan concept of the regulative principle, and he does so, all the while maintaining a principle of continuity, or analogy, between life in general and worship in particular. However, rather than establishing the degree of precision required in the Puritan principle, this concept of a regulative principle for life argues against the Puritan principle. That is, to argue that the regulation of worship is but a specific application of the regulation of life is to undermine the nature of the Puritan regulative principle of worship.

The force of this admission, namely that all of life is regulated, has not been lost on another proponent of the Puritan principle.[9] Michael Bushell, who would consider himself in agreement with Shepherd on the Puritan regulative principle, nonetheless rejects the analogy between the regulative principle of worship and the regulative principle for life. To the contrary, Bushell argues that the biblical requirements for worship differ in nature from those for life in general. He sees God's regulation of life in general as being far less demanding than his regulation of worship.

In order to understand Bushell's views accurately, one should note the following:

> In the religious worship of God, the primary governing principle is "whatsoever is not commanded, is forbidden." But this principle simply does not hold for life in general. An individual has a certain discretionary power in the ordering and formulating of his day-to-day activities, subservient to the general rules of Scripture, which he simply does not have when it comes to the self-conscious acts of worship. The Scriptures make it clear that within that realm the requirements are far more specific and far more rigorous.[10]

Thus, in Bushell's attempt to salvage the pedantic character of the regulative principle, he is willing to sacrifice what Shepherd sees as the covenantal character of life. That is, Shepherd views human beings in covenant relation to God as responsible for genuinely free, creative activity. Here, Shepherd is following in the tradition of Cornelius Van Til, who sees God's order, that is, his decree, as being the very basis for free, responsible human action, not the contradiction of that action. As Van Til expresses it,

> As Christians, we hold that determinate human experience could work to no end, could work in accordance with no plan, and could not even get under way, if it were not for the existence of the absolute will of God as portrayed in Scriptures. It is on this ground, then, that from the point of view of the necessity of the ethical life, we hold to the absolute will of God as the presupposition of the will of man. Looked at in this way, that which to many seems to be the greatest hindrance to human responsibility, namely, the conception of an absolutely sovereign God, becomes the very foundation of its possibility.[11]

Bushell refuses to buy into the formulation offered, for example, by Shepherd and Van Til, in order to avoid the logical implications of that position. Shepherd, of course, tries to maintain the strictness of the Puritan principle by referring to the regulative principle for worship as "the most pointed application of the regulative principle for life."[12] However, the main thrust of his argument is that as divine commands both principles partake of the same characteristics, "for all actions must be an expression of the love for God required of us."[13] Yet the Christian life is not regulated with the rigor that the Puritan regulative principle applies to worship. Bushell has rightly surmised that given Shepherd's view of broader and narrower aspects of God's regulation of life, it would be impossible to maintain the traditional Puritan regulative principle of worship.

BIBLICAL CONSIDERATIONS

The discussion linking the regulation of life and worship leads necessarily to a more pointed question, namely, whether it is proper to view all of life as worship. Bushell, for example, denies the legitimacy of this identification, preferring instead to see it as nothing more than figurative language.[14] However, adherence to the Puritan regulative principle of worship does not require a denial that all of life is worship. On the contrary, as one adherent of the Puritan principle has expressed it, "all of life is a service before the Lord."[15] The more pointed question, however, is whether there is a solid biblical basis for this identification. Is there a reasonable exegetical basis for describing all of life as worship? Indeed, the New Testament indicates that this is a legitimate concept.

While there are several words used for worship in the New Testament, they all share one thing in common.[16] Aside from references to Old Testament worship, which was by nature clearly sacral or cultic, the New Testament terminology has been desacralized.[17] "The terminological evidence means not only that any cultic understanding of Christian worship is out of the question, but also that there is no longer any distinction in principle between assembly for worship and the service of Christians in the world." That is, worship is no longer identified with the cult, but now is explained in general terms of "rendering service," not ministering in a priestly or sacrificial capacity.[18]

Two key word groups that indicate just this shift in New Testament thought are *leitourgeō/leitourgia* and *latreuō/latreia*. The biblical evidence for this interpretation is consistent. For example, in regards to the word *latreia*, the New Testament routinely uses this word (or its verbal form) to speak of noncultic activity when referring to Christian activity, as in Acts 24:14 or Romans 1:9.[19] Such *latreia* is based on "the inner worship of the heart by faith" and involves the presentation through the Spirit of the believer's "whole being."[20]

Consider Romans 12:1–2, where Paul exhorts the Roman Christians to present themselves as a living sacrifice, *thusian zōsan*, which he describes as their "reasonable service," *logikēn latreian*. Here, the believer metaphorically offers a sacrifice. "The service which Christians are to offer consists in the fashioning of their inner lives and their outward physical conduct in a way which plainly distinguishes them from the world and which corresponds to the will of God."[21] Or, as C. E. B. Cranfield has explained it, "The true worship which God desires embraces the whole of the Christian's life from day to day."[22]

Likewise, *leitourgia*, although occasionally incurring a cultic significance (e.g., Heb. 8:6 or Phil. 2:17), also acquires a spiritualized sense in which it stands for service of God in general. Originally, *leitourgia* was used as a technical term for "the priestly cultus."[23] However, the New Testament has largely changed the significance of this term, never employing it in a cultic sense to refer to a specifically Christian office or act. Of course, Old Testament concepts and figures are used in the New Testament to explain the significance of the Christ event, and at such times *lei-tourgeō* or a cognate is used. However, such use does not signify any priestly aspect to Christian worship. Instead, there are clear uses in the New Testament where all cultic significance has disappeared, such as Acts 13:2, Romans 15:27, and 2 Corinthians 9:12. Here, the word has come to stand for the service of God in general.[24]

Much more evidence could be cited, but the teaching of the New Testament with regard to worship is unambiguous.[25] A fundamental change has been ushered in with regard to the Old Testament. The New Testament knows no holy persons who substitutionally perform the service of God for the whole people of God, nor holy places and seasons or holy acts that create a distance between the cultus and the life of every day and every place. All members of the church have access to God (Rom. 5:2) and a share in the Holy Spirit. All of life is service to God; there is no "profane" area.

While there is not complete agreement over the treatment of every occurrence of the language of worship, there is a scholarly consensus that the language has clearly abandoned its Old Testament cultic orientation, for the Old Testament cult has been fulfilled in Christ. Now, cultic language is much more suited to describing the covenantal life of faith and obedience that every believer is called to offer as a "reasonable service" to God. "We too have a covenant, a priesthood, sacrifices, a tabernacle, circumcision, atonement, and feasts. But in our actual practice, there are great differences, for all of these institutions now exist in Christ and in him alone."[26]

Of course, this does not undermine the requirement for corporate worship in the New Testament, but provides a foundation for it. Indeed, the New Testament provides for the office of elder, and the teaching elder, who serves as minister of Word and sacrament, holds a special office ("worthy of double honor") in the church. Moreover, the Word, the sacraments of baptism and the Lord's

Supper, and prayer are means of grace, and should be central to the Lord's Day gathering of God's people. But the sacrifice we offer is a sacrifice of praise as we celebrate the one sacrifice of Jesus that forever takes away sin. There is something "special" about the Lord's Day gathering of God's people,[27] for corporate worship is a time of focused celebration, and collective offering of praise. But none of this should be separated sharply from the daily offering up of self in praise and thanksgiving, for all believers, "like living stones, are being built into a spiritual house to be a holy priesthood, offering spiritual sacrifices acceptable to God through Jesus Christ" (1 Peter 2:5).

THE WILL OF GOD AND WORSHIP

There is another important dimension to this issue. The will of God is sufficiently propounded in the Word of God, and the church is explicitly commanded to teach and observe all that Jesus has taught. The law of God, under one particular model, may be viewed as falling under two broad categories, apodictic and casuistic. Apodictic law "is characterized by its terseness and abruptness, and is an absolute command, apparently admitting no exceptions, usually making use of the second person sing[ular] of the future (either in the positive or negative form)."[28]

The other category, casuistic law, is essentially case law.[29] This type of law refers to examples or precedents that have occurred and have now entered into the law code as specific applications of the law. Of course, even a superficial survey of Old Testament law (and the New Testament, for that matter) reveals that God has not given to the church casuistic law for every contingency. Rather, he has given sufficient revelation, often in the form of absolute but general law (e.g., "You shall not murder," or "You shall not covet"). The effect is not to produce mechanical obedience to an infinitely extensive law code. Rather, this approach fosters wisdom through instruction in godly principles. Every believer, then, is able to evaluate the changing situations of life in terms of the requirement to "take captive every thought to make it obedient to Christ" (2 Cor. 10:5).

John Frame has addressed this particular dynamic:

> To discover the meaning of the facts is at the same time to discover the specific applications of the laws—applications that are as binding as the laws themselves. In studying the world, we discover in more and more detail what our obligations are. Or, to put it differently, the law itself commands us to live wisely—to live according to an understanding of reality.[30]

In wisdom, the Christian is to learn to think covenantally, responsibly, as a mature believer in the Lord.[31] This is not a license for unbounded freedom. It is, however, a charter for mature, thoughtful reflection on God's world from God's perspective.

It is just this same thoughtful, mature reflection that God demands in reference to corporate worship. Worship is regulated, even as life is regulated, based on the clear, sufficient teaching of Scripture, which sets boundaries and limits actions, but provides liberty and freedom of response within those parameters. Francis Schaeffer has pointed out that both form and freedom are grounded in creation and both must be asserted—in balance. "The Bible gives a world view that provides order and yet at the same time freedom. God's rules are like a perimeter fence. We must stay within that fence if we are to avoid getting messed up. But inside the fence we have an almost endless *variety of possibilities for freedom*. These touch every area of human life."[32]

The failure to appreciate both of these aspects in the history of worship—form and freedom, or spontaneity and uniformity—led to the unbearable tension in the Church of England. The attempt to resolve everything in favor of one side or the other of the balanced equation resulted, historically, in the Anglican-Puritan schism. Too much freedom resulted in the Anglican emphasis on the church's prerogative to determine the bounds of acceptable worship. Too much form resulted in the Puritan requirement limiting worship to that which is commanded. That same tension today is leading Presbyterians to movements of the left, "free liturgy," or of the right, "liturgical uniformity."

COVENANTAL CONSCIOUSNESS

Closely related to the above discussion are some ideas that Cornelius Van Til developed in expounding his view of Christian ethics. While it is clear that worship and ethics are distinct categories of thought and action, they are nonetheless inseparable.[33] Indeed, these categories are mutually related and reciprocally conditioned. Thus, the insights that Van Til has offered for the service of God in general—Christian ethics—may be related to worship in either of two ways. On the one hand, ethics may be related specifically to corporate, public worship by viewing worship simply as an application of Christian ethics. On the other hand, worship may be viewed as coextensive with Christian ethics, if worship is considered in its more general sense as descriptive of the entirety of the Christian life. However the particular relationship is viewed, there is a necessary connection.

Van Til expresses several important concepts in his discussion of Christian ethics, but four are clearly significant for the question of the regulation of worship. These four concepts are: (1) vicegerency, (2) self-realization, (3) individualization, and (4) analogical action. With regard to the first, Van Til notes that Adam was appointed God's vicegerent with dominion over the created order: "Man was created God's vicegerent and he must realize himself as God's vicegerent. There is no contradiction between these two statements. Man was created a character and yet he had to make

himself ever more of a character. So we may say that man was created a king in order that he might become more of a king than he
was."[34]

This relationship is best described as covenantal. Adam, as head
of the creation, was responsible for bringing all of creation together
to display the glory of God. This service by Adam on behalf of God
was to be "one central self-conscious sacrifice" unto God.[35] Thus,
he was created to rule over the rest of creation, not according to ab-
stract notions of dominion, but according to concrete conformity to
the will of God. Indeed, the command to rule is also a command
to exercise decision-making authority. The fall into sin, of course,
has had its effects on all aspects of human nature. However, the
mandate of God to exercise dominion has never been rescinded.
Further, by redemption, God once again enables man to be his
faithful servant and to rule over creation in justice and obedience.
And he does so without an endless list of rules and applications.

Second, although Adam was created with the necessary gifts
and abilities to perform this service, he was to improve himself by
service to the Lord.

> He was made a fit instrument for this work, but he must also
> make himself an ever better instrument for this work. He
> must will to develop his intellect in order to grasp more com-
> prehensively the wealth of the manifestation of the glory of
> God in this world. He must will to be an ever better prophet
> than he already is. He must will to develop his aesthetic ca-
> pacity, that is, his capacity of appreciation; he must will to be
> an ever better priest than he already is. Finally he must will
> to will the will of God for the whole world; he must become
> an ever better king than he already is. For this reason then the
> primary ethical duty for man is self-realization.[36]

Van Til makes several important observations. First, by willing
obedience to God, man was to become more spontaneous in his

response to changing circumstances. Second, man's will was to become increasingly "fixed in its self-determination." And third, man's will would increase in momentum as his responsibilities increased.[37] In other words, Adam was created to serve God, but not in a mechanical or rote fashion. Rather, gifted with abilities and placed under covenantal responsibility to God, he was to develop his ability to serve God as his will became more conformed to the will of God. This was to be accomplished, not by memorizing a rigid set of rules, but by becoming an obedient creature. Through the process of exercising dominion over an increasingly complex creation, man was to achieve his own self-realization, which resulted in a creature fully self-conscious, yet fully conformed to the will of God. Duty for man is self-realization.[38]

Third, the ongoing development of man would bring about individualization. No one would be under compulsion to act, but would act freely.[39] Continued obedience to God would increase the spontaneity of man's actions as his instincts and will, fallen but redeemed, are ever more yielded to doing the will of God.[40] Most importantly, there would be an opening up of the culture as individuals pursued their various vocations, using their talents for the glory of God. Van Til explains the importance of this concept: "Hence there would not be mere monotonous repetition in the kingdom of God. *There would be an inexhaustible variety. Individuality would be at a premium.* And no one would develop his individuality at the expense of others. The more anyone would develop his own individuality, the more he would give others an opportunity to develop their own individualities."[41] Thus, individuality is not hindered by conformity to the will of God, but is dependent upon it and liberated by it. Creativity is of the essence of the faithful exercise of dominion.[42]

Fourth, and final in our consideration, is Van Til's observation that man's dominion activity is *analogical* in character. Here Van Til argues that, although the kingdom of God is a gift to man, nonetheless man is responsible, ethically, for behavior that brings about the realization of the kingdom. "In theological terms we speak of this when we say, after Paul, that though it is God who worketh in us both to will and to do, yet we are to work out our own salvation with fear and trembling. Is there a conflict between them? Not at all. We can speak of the kingdom of God both as a *Gabe* [gift] and as an *Aufgabe* [task, or duty]."[43] For Van Til, such a construct is permissible because "it is of the very heart of theistic metaphysics to say that all human action is analogical action. Every act of a temporal being is based upon the creating and sustaining power of God. Even when man was in paradise his own life was a gift and the universe was a gift, and yet because of this very fact its development could also be a thing to strive after. Moral responsibility is impossible upon any other basis than that of the theistic idea of analogical action."[44] Thus, man as God's vicegerent, ever pursuing greater spontaneity and conformity to the will of God, increasingly differentiating his tasks and cultural achievements, truly would emulate God as his actions mimed the Creator.

The ramifications of these concepts for questions of life and worship should be apparent. Worship was never intended to consist in simple conformity to a comprehensive set of guidelines. Even in the Mosaic economy, filled with ceremonial and typical elements, basic to true worship was the exercise of dominion as faithful obedient creatures. Now, in the cultural diversity of the New Testament church, the occasion for exercising such stewardship has vastly increased.

Of course, such a concept of worship is fraught with tremendous burdens, as believers are charged with covenantal faithfulness along with cultural dominion. Nevertheless, life itself is covenantal and filled with the same opportunities for covenant faithfulness or covenant apostasy. Instead of creating fear or hesitancy, the implications of Van Til's ethical structures should be viewed rather as liberating. They provide freedom for the believer—not from obedience to the law of God—but for developing the principles of the law of God and applying them to every aspect of life, as worship, and every occasion of worship, as corporate, public event.

ADIAPHORA AND THE NEW TESTAMENT

Our earlier investigations established that one of the leading causes of conflict between Anglican and Puritan was the question of *adiaphora*. For the Anglican, there was a broad category of things deemed indifferent, and therefore suitable to be used if the church so willed. For the Puritan, the narrow if not nonexistent realm of *adiaphora* fell victim to an insistence on a positive biblical command for every essential part of worship. Our survey of Calvin's views on the regulation of worship established that he accepted, relative to later Puritanism, a broader area of things indifferent. Further, it is fair to say that with regard to *adiaphora*, Calvin and the later Anglicans were more faithful to the biblical evidence and the general Reformed consensus than were the Puritans. Given our examination of the biblical and theological basis for viewing all of life as worship, we have even more reason to look more closely at the related issue of *adiaphora*.

While any number of passages might prove appropriate to this discussion, only four will be considered here: Acts 16, Acts 21, Romans 14, and 1 Corinthians 8.

Acts 16

Acts 16:1–3 describes a situation that has bearing on the issue of *adiaphora*: "He [Paul] came to Derbe and then to Lystra, where a disciple named Timothy lived, whose mother was a Jewess and a believer, but whose father was a Greek. The brothers at Lystra and Iconium spoke well of him. Paul wanted to take him along on the journey, so he circumcised him because of the Jews who lived in that area, for they all knew that his father was a Greek." Here, the apostle Paul took young Timothy, the son of a mixed marriage, and had him circumcised before setting out on a missionary journey.

This may appear inconsistent on the part of Paul; after all, he warned the church in Galatia against circumcision. However, the circumstances were entirely different, and therein lies the relevance of this passage to the question of *adiaphora*. The problem in Galatia involved the very essence of the gospel. There certain "heretical teachers . . . taught that circumcision was necessary for salvation (5:2; 6:12ff.), and they accordingly demanded a maintenance of the ceremonial law of Moses, or at least the observation of days and months and seasons and years."[45] The situation with Timothy was not a matter of compulsion. Rather, Paul's action in circumcising Timothy was simply a matter of expediency. He "had Timothy circumcised out of consideration for the Jews of the region."[46]

Paul did not do this out of any lack of conviction. Rather, it was precisely his conviction that circumcision no longer had any religious significance that led him to undertake this action simply on the basis of expediency.[47] Circumcision, in light of the gospel and the progress of redemptive history, had entered into the realm of indifferent things—neither commanded nor prohibited. Therefore, if the use of an indifferent matter would be an asset in the work of the ministry, Paul was satisfied that it would be quite proper. It was done "for a practical purpose, and not a religious rite."[48] For Paul, then, even an Old Testament Jewish religious practice was indifferent, to be used or avoided depending on the needs of the church.[49]

Acts 21

In Acts 21:15–26, the apostle had entered into Jerusalem and found that distorted accounts of his ministry had been circulating. Rumor had it that Paul had been encouraging all Jews to abandon Jewish customs and live as Gentiles (v. 21). The advice to Paul was to demonstrate that he was not against the law by participating in a rite of purification in the temple. In verse 26 we see these words: "The next day Paul took the men and purified himself along with them. Then he went to the temple to give notice of the date when the days of purification would end and the offering would be made for each of them." The significance of this passage for the question of *adiaphora* is simply that Paul considered himself free to participate in a particular rite of Jewish purification as long as there was no compulsion and as long as there was a reasonable, practical need for such participation. Here, "Acts has described Paul as a Christian participating in Jewish customs that were not in conflict with Christ and his Gospel. Nothing in his letters suggests that he could not have participated in a Nazirite vow."[50]

The key to Paul's participation lies in two facts. First, there was no longer any binding religious obligation to participate in such a rite since Christ had fulfilled all elements of the ceremonial law (Col. 2:16–17). Second, there was no attempt to obligate him to observe the rite; instead, there was simply an appeal to circumstantial need and the edification of the church. Thus, for the sake of expediency Paul complied. F. F. Bruce's comment on this text is very helpful: "The ancestral customs were probably to him matters of use and wont, which he normally observed, and especially when doing so helped on his main object in life. But they were to him *religiously* indifferent."[51]

In both of these passages, then, we see Paul voluntarily practicing something that he clearly declares to be nonobligatory and unnecessary. For Paul, there was no inherent religious advantage to be gained by the actions, nor was there any inherent religious loss to be suffered by not performing the actions. He engaged in both acts of worship simply on the basis of expediency for the edification of believers in those particular situations.

R o m a n s   1 4

The third passage that makes reference to *adiaphora* is Romans 14. In this passage, it is clear that a conflict has arisen between two groups of believers, one that is "weak" in the faith and the other that is "strong" in the faith.[52] The exact occasion of the weakness that is referred to in this passage is unknown.[53] However, it is clear that the substance of the matter was that one group was convinced that to engage in certain practices, eating meat or observing days, was a matter of religious importance. Thus, there is "a scrupulos-ity with respect to the use of certain meats and drinks."[54] Cranfield summarizes the situation:

> The most probable explanation of the nature of the dis-agreement between the weak and the strong, to which this section refers, is that, whereas the strong had recognized that, now that He who is the goal and substance and in-nermost meaning of the OT law has come, the ceremonial part of it no longer requires to be literally obeyed, the weak felt strongly that a continuing concern with literal obedi-ence of the ceremonial law was an integral element of their response of faith to Jesus Christ, though their attitude was fundamentally different from that of the Judaizers of Gala-tians in that they did not think to put God under an obli-gation by their attempted obedience but only to express their faith.[55]

What is most significant in this passage is the apostle's concern with freedom of conscience in regard to both parties. While Paul may have been expected to take a position in favor of the strong, he instead treads a middle path, validating the necessity of personal conviction as the basis of action (v. 5). Indeed, at times a weak con-science may need further instruction in Christian freedom. John Murray notes the necessity of bringing "understanding and faith" to correspond with what is true. However, due consideration must be given to the state of the believer; "though things are indifferent in themselves the person is never in a situation that is indiffer-ent."[56]

Paul is explicit in affirming that nothing that God has created, or instituted, is of itself unclean.[57] Thus, those things which have neither been commanded nor forbidden are in essence indifferent, or *adiaphora*. The criterion of use or abstinence then becomes one's attitude toward the Lord. An individual may use a thing, participate in an action, or observe a practice—or not use, participate, or observe—depending upon one's own convictions and faith orientation.

Of course, Paul argues that both the weak and the strong have obligations to each other. The strong are not to impose their convictions on the weak; neither are the weak to judge and censure the strong. Rather, they are both to recognize that their differing convictions are in regard to "matters quite indifferent in themselves."[58] Murray summarizes the conclusion we must draw from this passage: "When we observe the hard and fast lines of distinction which God has established for us, and refuse to legislate on those matters that in themselves are not wrong, then we promote the interests of Christian ethics."[59] By way of application to our concerns here, this passage warns the church against requiring circumstances of worship that are otherwise not commanded, *and* prohibits the forbidding of circumstances of worship that are not otherwise condemned.

1 Corinthians 8

The fourth and final passage to be considered is 1 Corinthians 8. The key to this passage is verse 8: "But food does not bring us near to God; we are no worse if we do not eat, and no better if we do." The situation in Corinth that provoked this entire passage was the use of meats previously offered to idols as an act of worship and then purchased and consumed by believers. The strong believers, knowing idols to be nothing, were eating with a clear conscience. Weak believers, on the other hand, associated this eating with their former worship of idols and stumbled over the practice.[60] Here, then, Paul is concerned with two related problems. Clearly, there is the need to address the confusion that exists over liberty and expediency in the matter of eating the meat offered to idols. Yet Paul is concerned also with teaching about the nature of Christian liberty per se.

Concerning the question of Christian liberty and *adiaphora*,

Paul emphasizes that to eat or refrain from eating is of no religious significance in and of itself. Thus, from God's perspective, "we lose nothing by refraining from using our liberty in this matter, and we gain nothing by exercising it."[61] Similarly, Gordon Fee comments on verse 8, "Very likely, this reflects Paul's own position on being 'kosher,' that food, like circumcision, does not 'present us' to God. We are none the worse if we do not eat such food (as with not being circumcised) and we are no better if we do (as with being circumcised). Such are strictly matters of indifference to God."[62] For Paul, then, the issue of pleasing God is summed up quite simply: the use or nonuse of meat (or any other similar matter) is completely irrelevant. "It is the clean heart, and not clean food, that will matter."[63]

In response to the confusion that exists in Corinth over the eating of meat that had been offered to idols, Paul gives some guidance as well. Since the use or non-use of such meat is indifferent before God, are there any other considerations that must be entertained? Of course, Paul is concerned that there be a proper use of freedom with regard to indifferent matters. Hence, he cautions the strong believers against an intemperate use of their freedom in verses 9–13. But the fact that circumstances may determine expediency with regard to indifferent matters is compatible with the apostle's overall teaching on *adiaphora*. Indeed, the very nature of indifferent things makes their use or nonuse dependent on prevailing circumstances in the church. Personal benefits, balanced with the needs of the church in general, are the determining factors in the use of *adiaphora*.

These passages provide insight into the biblical teaching on *adiaphora*. By definition, an *adiaphoron* is in itself indifferent. Thus eating, drinking, observing days, or even circumcision, all of which had religious significance under the Mosaic economy, no longer have any religious significance per se. Therefore, there is nothing to be gained or lost in using them or refraining from their use. The factors that are determinative are the believer's own disposition (conscience) before God and the well-being of the congregation.

It may be true that today there are no circumstances that exactly duplicate those which Paul faced, but it is equally true that the principle of *adiaphora* is applicable to other questions that may arise in the context of the contemporary church. To such questions the answer must be that that Paul has already given: "One man considers one day more sacred than another; another man considers every day alike. Each one should be fully convinced in his own mind. He who regards one day as special, does so to the Lord. He who eats meat, eats to the Lord, for he gives thanks to God; and he who abstains, does so to the Lord and gives thanks to God" (Rom. 14:5–6).

ADIAPHORA AND THE REFORMED CONFESSIONS

Not only does the New Testament find ample room for the concept of *adiaphora*, but the consensus of the Reformation was that such a category was absolutely necessary to understand the role of the church in worship. While the following is not exhaustive, it is certainly representative of the various Reformation strains and confessional statements. *Adiaphora* was an official category in Lutheran thought as early as the Augsburg Confession in 1530.[64] However, in the definitive Formula of Concord, *adiaphora* receives a full exposition. In article 10, the Epitome addresses the question of rites and ceremonies "which are neither enjoined nor forbidden in the Word of God, but have been introduced into the Church merely for the sake of order and seemliness."[65] After stating the current issue, namely, conformity to papal impositions, the Epitome delineates the Lutheran position. In section 1, it says that ceremonies or rites, neither commanded nor forbidden, "are of themselves neither divine worship, nor even any part of divine worship."[66]

The Epitome makes further important statements regarding *adiaphora*. "We believe, teach, and confess that it is permitted to the Church of God any where on earth, and at whatever time, agreeably to occasion, to change such ceremonies, in such manner as is judged most useful to the Church of God and most suited to her edification."[67] The Lutheran testimony is that the church has authority to institute practices in worship according to the needs of the church. Sections 3 and 5 further establish principles that the consciences of the weak must not be violated, and that variations in worship should not be occasions for condemnation of one church by another.

The Belgic Confession, written by Guy de Brés, contains a section that is pertinent to our concerns. Article 32 reads as follows:

> In the mean time we believe though it is useful and beneficial that those who are rulers of the Church institute and establish certain ordinances among themselves for maintaining the body of the Church; yet they ought studiously to take care that they do not depart from those things which Christ, our only master, hath instituted. And, therefore, we reject all human inventions, and all laws which man would introduce into the worship of God, thereby to bind the conscience in any manner whatever. Therefore we admit only of that which tends to nourish and preserve concord and unity, and to keep all men in obedience to God.[68]

Here the confession makes a clear assertion that care must be taken in the institution of indifferent matters, allowing only those which further the well-being of the church.[69] Further, explicit warning is made against the binding of the conscience in any matter not commanded in Scripture. Thus a balanced approach to *adiaphora* is present in the document.

Written largely by John Knox, the Scotch Confession of Faith of 1560 might be expected to take a hard line with regard to *adi-*

aphora. However, the confession gives witness to the temporal character of ceremonies and the necessity of changing those ceremonies from time to time, as the church deems necessary. Here, in article 20, concerning the general councils of the church, the issue of worship is addressed:

> The uther wes [other was] for gude [good] policie, and ordour to be constitute and observed in the Kirk, quhilk [which], as in the house of God, it becummis *al things to be done decently and in ordour*. Not that we think that any policie and an ordour in ceremonies can be appoynted for al ages, times, and places: For as ceremonies, sik [such] as men have devised, ar bot temporall; so may and aucht they to be changed, when they rather foster superstition then that they edifie the Kirk using the same.[70]

Of course, it is clear that the abuses of the Roman Catholic Church are the major concern mentioned here. Nevertheless, Knox's incipient Puritanism is balanced with his catholicity, making allowance for change as the church deems necessary.

The Second Helvetic Confession, written by Heinrich Bullinger, was published in 1566. Despite the strictures normally associated with Zurich, there is testimony here to *adiaphora*. While arguing strongly for adherence to the pattern given by the Lord himself, there is yet admission of an area of freedom in matters of worship. Chapter 17 says,

> Furthermore, we teach that it is carefully to be marked, wherein especially the truth and unity of the Church consists, lest that we either rashly breed or nourish schisms in the Church. It consists not in outward rites and ceremonies, but rather in the truth and unity of the Catholic faith. . . . And, therefore, we read in the ancient writers that there were manifold diversities of ceremonies, but that

these were always free; neither did any man think that the unity of the Church was thereby broken or dissolved. We say, then, that the true unity of the Church does consist in several points of doctrine, in the true and uniform preaching of the Gospel, and in such rites as the Lord himself has expressly set down.[71]

The Thirty-Nine Articles of the Church of England provide the most expansive discussion of *adiaphora*, the power of the church, and the role of conscience. In article 20, "Of the aucthoritie of the Church," we read,

The Church hath power to decree Rites or Ceremonies, and aucthoritie in controuersies of fayth: And yet it is not lawfull for the Church to ordayne any thyng that is contrarie to Gods worde written, neyther may it so expounde one place of Scripture, that it be repugnant to another. Wherefore, although the Churche be a witnesse and a keper of holy writ: yet, as it ought not to decree any thing agaynst the same, so besides the same, ought it not to enforce any thing to be beleued for necessitie of saluation.[72]

The Thirty-Nine Articles further explain that it is acceptable for traditions and ceremonies to vary from place to place, that such ceremonies may be changed according to the cultural context, and that the church has authority in matters not contrary to Scripture to establish, change, or remove rites and ceremonies according to their edification of the church.[73]

Finally, even the Westminster Confession of Faith, in an indirect fashion, speaks of *adiaphora* in chapter 20, section 2 on "Christian Liberty." "God alone is Lord of the conscience, and hath left it free from the doctrines and commandments of men, which are in any thing contrary to his Word; or beside it, if matters of faith or worship."[74] Evidently, the primary interest here is negative, noting that the conscience of the Christian is free and not subject to human constraints. While it is clear that this is the primary intent of the passage, the words themselves indicate that there are matters of indifference, matters that are "beside" the Word. Of course, the confession then proceeds to forbid just such voluntary acts of worship in chapter 21, section 1 ("Of Religious Worship and the Sabbath Day").

In these documents, there are various emphases and teachings. Some are more indirect, while others are more explicit. Nonetheless, there is a consensus among these major Reformation confessions that there are matters neither commanded nor forbidden that may be used, established, changed, or removed by the church, depending upon the exact situation the church faces. This is consonant with the teachings of the New Testament on the nature of worship and the concept of *adiaphora*. Further, we may well conclude that much of the turmoil in the Anglican-Puritan controversy, as well as much of the confusion in the history of Presbyterian worship, could have been avoided by incorporating these two things: (1) a recognition that all of life is worship and is regulated along the lines of covenantal faithfulness, and (2) a healthy respect for and sober use of the concept of *adiaphora* as applied to the question of circumstances.

Chapter 8

IN LIGHT OF THE COVENANT

*A*ll that has preceded has been helpful in determining that the regulative principle of worship, as formulated by the Puritans and as adopted by the divines at the Westminster Assembly, is unworkable. More importantly, it is simply not the teaching of Scripture. Does this mean, then, that worship is a matter of complete freedom, subject to individual tastes or corporate denominational dictates? Or is it possible to integrate an expanded view of *adiaphora* (circumstances) into the overall context of Reformed worship? The important fact is that although the Puritan regulative principle has been found wanting, this does not mean that the Scriptures fail to give guidance in regards to worship. Surely the Puritan emphasis that worship should be regulated by the Word of God was on the right track. The Bible does provide parameters for acceptable worship. It does give guidelines for regulating the public, corporate worship of the church, and it does provide parameters for properly using those matters deemed indifferent.

The immediate problem is one of terminology. Having granted that the Bible does regulate worship, what name should we give to the biblical principles that regulate worship? The historic phrase, the "regulative principle," presents itself as an obvious possibility. It has the advantage of being straightforwardly descriptive; after all, we are seeking to determine biblical principles for regulating worship. The problem is that this phrase already has a well-defined meaning in the history of the church and in the theology of worship. It is identified, specifically, with the Puritan understanding of the regulation of worship. Furthermore, there are many problems related to worship in the Presbyterian churches today that may be directly attributed to the equivocation and ambiguity that already surround the phrase "regulative principle of worship." To attempt now to redefine it would simply confound the issue further.

Another possible name would be the "biblical principle of worship." This has the advantage of indicating agreement with and dependence upon the Scriptures. Nevertheless, it has a drawback as well, for the term "biblical" is often used today in contexts where obscurantism reigns. Thus to define something as "biblical" often does more to obfuscate an issue than to clarify it. A further drawback is the unfortunate fact that in the history of the church, "biblical" worship has been the rallying cry of certain Anabaptist groups who are clearly in disagreement with the Reformed faith and the principles that will be argued below.

Perhaps, in light of the discussions above, a better term to give to our suggested approach to worship is the "covenantal principle of worship." The advantages of this are obvious. First, the name places itself squarely within the context of Reformed consideration, since by definition Reformed theology is very much concerned with covenants and covenantal relations. The covenant formula, "I will be your God, and you will be my people," sets forth both promise and obligation in terms of covenant relationship. Second, this term clearly implies responsibility and certainly provides no room for any notion of simple, mechanical conformity. Indeed, the obligation of the covenant requires faithful, responsible, and intentional obedience to covenant precepts and principles.

Third, it is clearly distinguishable from other approaches to worship and avoids the danger of confusion. Thus, the "covenantal principle of worship" will be the name given to the regulation of worship advocated in the following pages.

We now face the task of giving substance to this phrase. Having acknowledged the Puritan regulative principle of worship to be flawed, we must now offer something in its place. In offering the covenantal principle of worship, it will be necessary to outline the parameters of its operation. These parameters are intended to be biblical in their basis and faithful to the Reformed tradition, particularly as expressed in the thought of John Calvin.

First, and most obviously, the covenantal principle of worship includes all those elements of worship that are clearly commanded in Scripture. At this point, the covenantal principle of worship is identical with the Puritan regulative principle. This would include what is positively commanded, such as praying, celebrating the sacraments, preaching, and singing of Psalms. Even as the Westminster Confession of Faith (1.6) speaks of those things "expressly set down in scripture," even so the covenantal principle of worship agrees with this assertion.

Second, and also in accordance with the Puritan regulative principle, the covenantal principle of worship includes all those things as well which "by good or necessary consequence may be deduced from Scripture" (Westminster Confession of Faith, 1.6). Thus, whatever is required by Scripture, or is a necessary, logical corollary of the teaching of Scripture, is affirmed as a part of covenantal worship and must be observed by the church. J. J. von Allmen, in a rather lengthy summary, has provided a synopsis of the elements necessary for worship to fulfill the most basic of biblical requirements:

> The NT marks the limits within which, with more or less felicity and obedience, Christian worship can truly be carried out as Christian worship. These limits are as follows:

first, the assembly must take place in the name of Jesus
Christ, to celebrate His victory and invoke His presence.
The intention of the celebrant must be to celebrate the
Christian cult. Secondly, this cult must enable the faithful
to persevere in the teaching of the apostles; next it must enable them, at the breaking of the bread, to communicate
with the body of Christ; fourthly, it must gather up the
prayers of the Church and offer them to God; finally, it
should be an assembly of men and women who are not just
juxtaposed as at the cinema, but committed to a way of life
in common. These last four characteristics make possible
the first.[1]

Third, and most significant for our discussion, the covenantal
principle of worship includes the freedom to worship in any manner warranted by the Scriptures. That is, the covenantal principle
of worship says that whatever is consistent with the Scriptures is acceptable in worship. Here is where the major difference with the
Puritan formula appears. For the Puritan, all worship was either
commanded or unlawful. If commanded, it was either directly
commanded (or logically necessary; thus essential) or indirectly
commanded, by general principle and Christian prudence (and
therefore circumstantial).

For the Puritan, the circumstantial alone may be viewed as *adiaphora*; but the circumstantial was so unduly restricted as to rule
out, in effect, the concept of indifferent things. Here, in the
covenantal principle of worship, there are still two categories: commanded, by direct precept or example (and therefore necessary),
and indirectly commanded, or governed by general principle and
Christian prudence (and therefore circumstantial *and indifferent*).
But the covenantal principle of worship insists that the second category must be given its due to include the broad range of *adiaphora*, things neither commanded nor forbidden, but governed
by the light of covenant faithfulness.

In other words, the concept of *adiaphora* expands our understanding of circumstances while leaving the concept of elements intact.[2] Without the concept of *adiaphora*, the Presbyterian churches have found themselves engaged in endless disputes about words. By refusing to acknowledge the breadth of circumstances, Presbyterians have continued to fight over definitions, arguing about such issues as whether the use of musical instruments is an element or a circumstance, or whether it is appropriate to have an Easter or Christmas service. Indeed, these things are *circumstances* of worship. For example, an Easter service is nothing more than the worship of God's people on Easter Sunday, with the usual elements of worship contextualized or conditioned by the circumstances of that particular Sunday.

This same thinking applies to the issue of ceremonies in the church. There is nothing in the Scriptures that tells us how to admit new members into the church. In many evangelical Presbyterian churches, this is done through instruction by the pastor and/or elders, an interview with the session for a profession of faith, and public recognition in the corporate worship service of the church. Is it not obvious that confirmation may accomplish exactly the same goal? Often, confirmation involves instruction by the pastor and/or elders, an interview with the session for a profession of faith, and a public prayer, often accompanied by the laying on of hands. Calvin thought this practice to be most consistent with Scripture, and so it seems to me.

As has been established in chapter 4, expanding the concept of circumstances to include *adiaphora*, in addition to those matters deemed essential, is consistent with John Calvin's view of worship. Also, as established by the biblical and theological principles discussed in chapters 5 and 6, such an approach to worship is in accord with the principles of covenant relationship. Further, as von Allmen explains, there is an abundance of opportunity for fleshing out specifics within the general limits established in Scripture: "To be Christian, worship must proceed within these limits, and whatever can be legitimately placed within them, whatever is not contradicted by them . . . can claim the right of being a *Christian* liturgical expression."[3] However, the biblical and theological principles that have been discussed also make it clear that *not everything* is an acceptable circumstance or a matter of indifference in worship. Therefore, some effort must be made to clarify further the boundaries, the parameters that circumscribe what may be freely used to constitute acceptable worship.

Before enumerating the various parameters for the covenantal principle of worship, certain preliminary remarks are necessary. First, although this work seeks to redirect the focus of worship, it does not answer every question that might arise. That is, further reflection and additional insights into historical, biblical, and theological data will lead to refining and expanding the parameters given here. While there are many reasons to believe that the direction described here is sound, all human efforts at theologizing are ultimately tentative. Thus, these proposals should be viewed as heuristic and not definitive. Second, not everyone will agree on how to apply the various parameters described. While the parameters themselves may be clear, it is inevitable that there will be some disagreement on the appropriate application of these guidelines to individual situations. This should not be a cause for despair, but an occasion for further dialogue.

Third, situations may arise in which there is disagreement over which guideline takes precedence over another. For example, one who comes from a traditional Reformed perspective will be more likely to give greater weight to simplicity, while someone from a Pentecostal background might prefer to emphasize liberty.[4] The following parameters are not listed in any particular order of importance, nor should they all be perceived to be equally important. Therefore, some guidelines are less forgiving when violated than others. With these warnings before us, we now move to consider the individual parameters that together constitute the covenantal principle of public, corporate worship in the church.

WORSHIP THAT IS SIMPLE

The first guideline of the covenantal principle of worship is simplicity. This is one of the obvious implications of Jesus' words in John 4:23–24: "Yet a time is coming and has now come when the true worshipers will worship the Father in spirit and truth, for they are the kind of worshipers the Father seeks. God is spirit, and his worshipers must worship in spirit and in truth." The term "simplicity" faces the immediate danger of being misunderstood because of its peculiar use by the Puritans. However, simplicity is not here a synonym for spirituality, as opposed to materiality. Neither should it be interpreted to mean that worship should appeal only to the mind (Gk. *nous*), be funneled only through the mind, or prohibit the use of the body, in movement, in touch, in smell, or in taste. Rather, simplicity as used here has a much richer significance.

First, worship that is acceptable today is worship that is done in a New Covenant context. While this does not exclude the Old Testament as normative in matters of worship, it does mean that certain particulars of the Old Testament are no longer applicable. Even as the unfolding of revelation and the progress of redemptive history have moved onward, two closely linked phenomena have occurred.[5] On the one hand, revelation has increased in an ongoing organic unfolding so that we possess greater knowledge and insight today than the Old Covenant people of God did. On the other hand, with the coming of Christ, this fullness of revelation has fulfilled the typological aspects of the Old Covenant, so that the pageantry of Old Testament worship is now passé. Thus, New Testament worship, relative to Old Testament worship, is simple.

Second, to explain this principle another way, New Testament worship is preeminently Spiritual worship, that is, worship in and of the Spirit. As has been noted, to speak of worship as Spiritual is not to oppose spirituality to materiality. Rather, it is an affirmation that we worship in the Spirit, for the people of God today are already partakers of the coming age. As Geerhardus Vos has explained this concept,

> The Spirit is viewed as pertaining specifically to the future life, nay as constituting the substantial make-up of this life, and the present possession of the Spirit by the believer is regarded in the light of an anticipation. The Spirit's proper sphere is according to this the world to come; from there He projects Himself into the present, and becomes a prophecy of Himself in His eschatological operation.[6]

Thus, New Covenant worship is preeminently worship in the Spirit, under the guidance of the Spirit, by the power of the Spirit.[7]

Third, simple worship is that which has direction and inner coherence. It is worship that "is in the first instance the opposite not of complexity but rather of diffuseness."[8] Again, this does not mean a bare-bones minimalism either in rite or ceremony. Rather, this "condition of true worship is a respect for the structure controlling the relations between the various parts of the cult, in an arrangement which shows that the cult progresses toward its culminating point, and that, having reached it, it is strengthened by it for the purpose of afterwards witnessing in the world."[9]

There is little likelihood that a consensus will be achieved on the exact limits of simplicity. Societies where nonverbal means of communication have been highly developed will appreciate a greater role for sign and symbol. Cultures where artistic achievement has developed significantly will have an aesthetic emphasis that differs significantly from those where such development has been hindered. Church communities where an openness to Pneumatic phenomena has been the tradition will be more open to whole-person worship than will those whose tradition lies more along the lines of didactic, teaching-oriented worship. These variables will affect the circumstances of worship. Nevertheless, every ecclesial community must take simplicity seriously, even if there is not complete agreement on its significance and application.

WORSHIP THAT IS ORDERLY

Orderliness is not only commanded as a criterion for acceptable New Testament worship (1 Cor. 14:40), but it is also one of the most basic themes in God's dealings with mankind. First, order is a necessary characteristic of acceptable worship because God himself is a God of order. The world that God created was a perfect creation, with balanced ecosystems providing for every possible need of human existence. As Francis Schaeffer has stated it,

> The universe has order. It is not chaos. One is able to proceed from the particulars of being to some understanding of its unity. One is able to move ever deeper into the universe and not come upon a precipice of incoherence. We find this emphasized in Genesis 1, which points out that God made all these things to produce after their own kind. Here is order. And so it is with the God of Scripture. He is not the philosophic other, nor the impersonal everything, nor that which is chaotic or random. He is a God who is (and I use this word carefully and worshipfully) a *reasonable* God.[10]

Second, order is associated with man by virtue of creation and participation in God's dominion over the world.[11] Thus, the general task of cultivation and the more specific task of cult both are to be characterized by obedience to God's law-word. Originally Adam was placed in the garden to maintain the order that was already established. Now, on account of the fall, redeemed man is called to restore order in a world where the chaos of lawlessness threatens to overwhelm the remnants of order. In other words, the cultural mandate is binding and has tremendous implications for the type of worship acceptable to God. Order is not optional; it is inherent in creation itself.[12]

Third, true orderliness is not necessarily inimical to freedom.[13] Rather, in worship, freedom is the expression of creativity, the harnessing of aesthetic impulses, and the deliberate ordering of religious expression within the boundaries of what is consistent with decent, orderly action. Robert Morey, commenting on Paul's instructions to the Corinthian church, observes: "Paul does not refer the Corinthians to a prescribed order of service revealed from God. He points them instead to a mature and responsible exercise of their priestly freedom in the non-essential aspects of worship."[14]

Orderliness, then, is concomitant with freedom, not inimical to it. Indeed the demands of orderliness point us toward a goal. Worship that is orderly is worship that is directed, coherent, and thoughtful. Such worship is anything but uniform, for diversity is grounded in the concept of order. As Vern Poythress says, "From creation onward, God intended that the human race should develop with a diversity of individuals. Even apart from the Fall, different people would have had different gifts and different experiences, so that one person's insights into the truth would complement those of another."[15] Thus, from creation, God has provided for creativity, individuality, and spontaneity within the bounds of created order. Worship that is orderly may exist in styles as diverse as charismatic worship or High Church liturgy. What is essential is that orderliness be uniformly pursued, even as its practice remains diversely applied.

WORSHIP THAT IS FREE

Essential to any genuine worship is the concept of liberty, or freedom. This concept may be defined in individual or ecclesial terms. First, we will consider the liberty of the individual. For the individual, the concept of liberty frees the believer from any coercive act on the part of the church. In other words, there must be freedom from the imposition of any act of worship that is not divinely commanded. Essentially, we are arguing here for liberty of conscience.

Historically, this has been a sore point for many believers of tender conscience. If the Puritans were wrong to restrict the use of *adiaphora* and narrow the range of circumstances (and they were), then, likewise, the Anglicans were guilty of imposing forms of worship that violated the consciences of many godly people. The question as to whether the conscience is properly informed is, in this context, irrelevant. What is absolutely important is that the conscience of every believer be respected and no one be forced to engage in an act of worship that, for conscience' sake, is deemed unacceptable. Paul has argued in Romans 14:23 that "everything that does not come from faith is sin."[16] For any believer to be coerced into doing something against conscience is tantamount to being forced to sin. Thus, the authority of the church is limited. Although a particular circumstance of worship is within the bounds of the covenantal principle of worship, if it is not specifically commanded or necessarily deduced from specific commands, it must not be imposed and made mandatory, although it may be observed voluntarily.

With regards to ecclesial freedom, the fact is that each congregation, within the bounds of the covenantal principle of worship, has the right to determine its own particular style or emphasis in worship. Thus, a New Life–model congregation, which encourages spontaneity and sharing, may indeed tailor its worship service, within the bounds of covenantal regulation, to support a free style of worship. Likewise, a High Church–model congregation has freedom to structure its liturgy according to historic forms, responses, and litanies, as long as it is faithful to all the other guidelines of the covenantal principle. As Howard Hageman explains, "The basic principle of Reformed worship . . . asserts that there is not and cannot be one liturgy for the Reformed church, valid at all times and in all places."[17]

Of course, this freedom also brings with it a weighty responsibility. To say that all worship styles are legitimate does not mean that every style of worship is equally worthy in every regard. For example, free worship may very well have certain advantages in terms of fellowship and mutual concern. However, it is also the case that free worship often suffers from a lack of historicity or catholicity. From another perspective, worship that may be more successful in integrating historic or catholic rites and ceremonies may need to consider ways to achieve openness and mutual encouragement more completely.[18] Thus, while it is possible to validate many worship styles, the freedom to use those styles does not absolve their proponents from the obligation to learn from others whose worship is valid as well. A spirit of openness and a willingness to be self-critical will enable adherents of all legitimate worship styles to identify their strong points and to reconsider their weak ones.

WORSHIP THAT GLORIFIES AND EDIFIES

There are two closely related lines of movement in worship, the vertical and the horizontal. Since we are to glorify God in everything we do (1 Cor. 10:31), how much more should we glorify him in our worship! Furthermore, we should worship in such a way as to edify our fellow believers.[19] Worshipers, then, need to go beyond themselves both vertically and horizontally, focusing not on the benefits they are to receive, but on the benefits they are to give.

First and foremost, worship must glorify God. To do this, there must be an awareness that the One being worshiped is "the almighty and ever-living God who is transcendent, the God who pervades the limitless universe. It is intensely sobering to realize that we worship the God who is 'wholly other,' the Almighty Creator, the Holy One, the King and Ruler of all."[20] Of course, this is not intended to deny God's immanence, for we would be unable to worship a being who was only "beyond." Rather, this is simply a reminder that in worship we are continually to focus on who God is and what he has done for us. God created his people to bring him glory, and this should be the believer's highest goal.[21]

Significantly, we serve a God who delights in blessing us. There is every reason to expect that even as the believer is called by God to glorify his majesty, there will be resultant personal benefits that return to God's faithful people. These reflexive benefits should not be the primary motivation in worship, but they should be anticipated in faith as the Divine-human dialogue transpires through the service of worship.[22]

The second line of movement, essential but subordinate to the first, is the edification of fellow believers. "If worship had only a vertical dimension and we witnessed only to God, then our pilgrimage would end here. But worship has a horizontal dimension: we witness to one another in the church and to a lost world outside the church. It is not enough that *I* am transformed by worship; I must also help to transform *others*, and I should allow others to be used by God to transform me."[23] Now, it is most important to remember that "edification does not mean 'good feelings.'"[24] Because it is very easy for a church to embrace particular acts, rites, ceremonies, or practices for reasons that are not legitimate, a distinction must be made between edification and entertainment, or edification and enjoyment.

While it is true that legitimate worship may be enjoyable, it must not be *only* enjoyable. All true worship must tend toward building up the body of Christ (1 Cor. 14:26). As Ronald Allen and Gordon Borror have explained it, true worship ought to be multifaceted, so that "when we worship, we edify; when we edify, we evangelize; when we evangelize, we worship."[25] It is not enough that one enjoy worship. True worship will build up the body of believers, and there is every reason to expect that such worship will have the reflex action of increasing joy and bringing satisfaction to the worshiper.

WORSHIP THAT IS CATHOLIC

Another guideline that should inform Reformed worship is the biblical concept of catholicity. Not only is catholicity embedded in the church's collective consciousness due to centuries of development, but it is also a concept that is found in the pages of the New Testament. The impetus for catholicity is found in Jesus' parting words to the church. He gives the Great Commission to his followers to make disciples of *all* nations (Matt. 28:19–20). Later, by way of application, Paul appeals to the Corinthians to conform their worship practices to the pattern that is found "in all the congregations of the saints" (1 Cor. 14:33).[26]

While there is some confusion regarding the exact practices that Paul wishes to bring into conformity, the desire for catholicity itself is certain.

> This particular appeal . . . is an indication to the Corinthians that their view of tongues and spirituality that has allowed this disorderly conduct is out of keeping with what God is doing elsewhere through the gospel. They are marching to their own drum; Paul is urging them not only to conform to the character of God, but also to get in step with the rest of his church.[27]

As Charles Hodge comments, the problem with the church at Corinth was that they were acting "contrary to established usage."[28] In this passage Paul gives concrete meaning to his teaching in 1 Corinthians 12 that the body of Christ is one, and whatever affects one member has effect upon all other members.

This emphasis on catholicity requires a certain attitude of openness on the part of those who are Reformed. As Richard B. Gaffin Jr. has stated, "What Reformed believers have in common with 'everyone who calls on the name of the Lord' (Rom. 10:13) is more basic than the differences, because above all they all share in Christ, and Christ is not divided (I Cor. 1:13)."[29] Not only is openness required, but a certain amount of humility is necessary as well. Reformed believers

> will not allow their confidence to lead them to suppose that they have cornered all truth or to obscure that they, too, only "see in a mirror dimly" (I Cor. 13:12). They will not at all be surprised, but grateful and delighted, to learn from and be edified by those in other traditions. At stake here is the capacity of the Reformed tradition to *grow*, so that in our day, "the Reformed church is always reforming" is something more than an empty slogan.[30]

Thus, there must be a willingness to learn from others, a willingness to be taught by the entire breadth of the Christian tradition.

Such an openness to other traditions will not be achieved easily. Nevertheless, the fact remains that even those whose traditions are most at variance with the Reformed probably have in some sense reproduced an aspect of the truth that the Reformed churches would be wise to consider. As Vern Poythress reminds us, "By looking for the 'grain of truth' even in some bad idea, we can sometimes find a starting point for a new perspective or a piece of truth that we ourselves had overlooked."[31] By way of illustration, the more free-flowing, Pentecostal churches must entertain the fact that there is something valuable in Episcopalian, High Church worship. *Mutatis mutandis*, the High Church advocates must recognize that there is some value in the free-flowing style of worship preferred by their Pentecostal brothers and sisters.

More basically, Protestants in general should be able to learn from the traditions of the Roman Catholic and Eastern Orthodox churches. After all, does not the sacramental focus of the Roman Catholic Church have something to say to Presbyterians whose worship, sadly enough, all too frequently has been desacramentalized? And does not the Orthodox tradition of mystery have something to contribute to the churches of the Reformation and their tendency toward intellectualized, overly didactic worship? Worship that is catholic requires the willingness to hear the truth contained in other traditions, even when that truth has been obscured by nonbiblical accretions.

One other aspect of catholicity needs to be elucidated. Thus far catholicity has been used in the sense of breadth. However, there is a linear or longitudinal sense of catholicity that reminds us that the church today is connected to the church of the apostles, the fathers, the martyrs, and the Reformers of over two thousand years of history. Von Allmen observes, "In its worship the Church bears witness that it unites the centuries, refusing to allow what is past to fall into oblivion, or what is promised to fade into illusion."[32] Thus, the church must seek to retain what is valuable, transforming its practice where necessary, but always with the sense of historical continuity. True catholicity, then, would find legitimate points of contact in worship, not only in the breadth of tradition present today, but in the riches of the liturgical tradition of the church.[33]

Indeed, there is much to be gained from the catholic tradition of the church, and much that is valuable to be gleaned from the practices of the entire church.[34] As Hageman has stated it, "Whatever in the ecumenical church is consonant with their Biblical and Reformed loyalties, is there for the Reformed churches to enjoy."[35] Worship that is truly catholic will seek to employ "whatever is true, whatever is noble, whatever is right, whatever is pure, whatever is lovely, whatever is admirable" (Phil. 4:8) regardless of its source, to building up God's people and the greater glory of God.

Worship That Is Culturally Sensitive

One of the paramount concerns in liturgical circles today is cultural sensitivity. Indeed, we are all more aware of the role that culture plays in our outlook on life.[36] In the past this was not the case. Instead, Reformed theologians were often guilty of absolutizing principles of worship that had been determined in the reactionary setting of Reformation/post-Reformation European polemics. Too often plainness and simple uniformity were understood to be normative.[37] Here cultural factors displaced the true center of Reformed liturgy, and in the passing of time became identified with truly Reformed worship.

It is imperative to separate the center or genius of Reformed liturgy from any particular cultural manifestation. "The controlling idea in Reformed worship is that God acts in worship and that we are not to hold God's actions at arm's length but to appropriate them into our innermost being. Worship is a meeting between God and his people, a meeting in which both parties act—God as the initiator and we as the responders."[38]

It is at this point that the possibility of cultural diversity plays an important part. The two sides of worship may be viewed as (1) God's initiative of grace, as proclaimed by the minister of the Word, elders, or laypersons on God's behalf to the congregation, and (2) the response of the people to that initiative, as led by the worship leader or leaders. Significantly, the forms that such Christian proclamation and response take do not participate in some supratemporal norm. Rather, "each worshiping community must seek to tell and act out the story and then respond to it in a way that is appropriate to its own culture. The context for worship must be in keeping with the cultural context. We need to know what is essential to worship and then we need to prayerfully contextualize it."[39] Simply put, the church must ever be alert to the danger of confusing timeless truth with its temporal manifestation.

After all, change in worship has been part of God's ongoing

plan of redemption. Even Scripture itself is filled with changes in worship from the patriarchal stage to the Mosaic, from the Mosaic to the Davidic, and from the Davidic to the New Covenant.[40] The biblical imperative for the church in relation to culture, then, is adaptation and transformation, redeeming that which is "noble and wholesome."[41] As long as the church is in the world, this will be a necessary part of her responsibility. "As a pilgrim people we ought to take more seriously the realization that our present forms or patterns are not the ultimate forms. From time to time we must fold up our tents and move on—but only when we are convinced that our move is obedient to the Word of God."[42]

The church, then, must be able to relate the truths of Scripture, particularly the positive commands regarding worship (together with the covenant principles that govern *adiaphora*), to the context in which an indigenous culture exists. As one writer has stated it, "When worship practice is consistent with life, worship will be relevant."[43] The genius of Reformed liturgy is revealed every time cultural adaptation of the liturgy is achieved.

WORSHIP THAT IS BALANCED

For want of a better description, this particular guideline may be referred to as balance. While all of the Christian life should be balanced, we must make two specific points regarding balance in reference to worship. There should be balance (1) between Word and symbol, and (2) between Word and Sacrament. That is, because of the nature of humanity, symbolism plays an important role along with didactic or simply verbal elements in worship. Furthermore, while sacraments are more than symbols, they may be viewed as the most focused point of symbolism in worship.

The fact is that all of humanity experiences the import of symbolism, much of which is related to the human body and its orientation in the world.

> Throughout the human race, the top and bottom, the right and left, the inside and outside of the body, and facing water, earth, wind, or fire are "figures" that enable man to speak— think— make the transexperimental world: life-death, heaven-hell, power-weakness, etc. The liturgy likewise is entirely structured by these bodily-cosmic figures: descent into–coming up from the waters of baptism; eating-and-drinking-together in the eucharistic meal; listening to–response to the Word; calling together–coming together–dispersal of assemblies, etc. We can never completely free ourselves of these figures. They affect every human being and are in a sense universal.[44]

Significantly, God has made use of such natural symbols in the church, and the church would be foolish to deny the power and influence such symbols contain.

Indeed, many of the problems that have occurred in theological anthropology have arisen because of the same impulses that would deny the value and role of symbol. Humans, according to the Scripture, are a unity, not a composite. Moreover, humans are a diversity as well, having "several dimensions or spheres of life" so that we may relate to the material world and to the spiritual world.[45] Thus, attempts to reduce humanity to only materialist aspects, or to free humans by identifying them with the spirit that is imprisoned in their bodies, are all notions that are pagan in orientation and not Christian. Neither a reductionist approach to humanity nor a composite approach satisfies the biblical data.

Another way of explaining this would be to note that humans are rational beings, but they are more than rational beings. Humans consist of intellect, but they are more than intellect, for they have will and emotions as well. Humans are creatures of the senses as well as of the mind. No one is perfectly balanced, and some will inevitably give a greater role to the emotions, while others may limit their affections by giving reign to the intellect.[46] Regardless of the particular orientation of an individual, the fact remains that the believer operates on all levels, seeing, hearing, tasting, smelling, touching, thinking, rejoicing, sorrowing. Thus, a balanced service of worship will speak to the mind, but it will also speak to the heart, to the emotions, to the will.[47]

Truth, then, can be communicated in worship not only through verbal explanations, but also through movement, posture, music, drama, art, and the wise use of sacred space and sacred time.[48] While there should be no compulsion in the matter, many in the church have experienced humility and submission through the act of kneeling in prayer. Others have rejoiced and exulted in the Lord by lifting up their hands to heaven, acting out what is transpiring at a deeper level. The bright, flowing banners used in some churches emphasize important aspects of God's redemption, or highlight special seasons in the Christian year.

The positioning of the pulpit, table, and font often tells as much about a church's worship as does the sermon or bulletin. Robert Webber has commented on the importance of the symbolic, particularly the return of aesthetics to worship:

> The historic argument for the use of the arts in worship is grounded in the incarnation. The claim is that God, by becoming a [human] person, sanctified physical and material reality as a vehicle for spiritual presence. He comes to us through flesh and blood. Why, then, shouldn't we accept appropriate art forms as visible means through which a spiritual reality becomes present or through which we offer praise?[49]

All Reformed believers will agree on the importance of word in worship. After all, the centrality of *The Word* is the great legacy of all Protestants.[50] However, not all will agree on where to place the fulcrum to balance word and symbol. Such disagreement is to be expected and not to be regretted. As each congregation adapts itself to the guidelines of Scripture, with sensitivity to the predominant modes of thinking, learning, and communicating present in the congregation, there will be differences of emphasis. The key, however, lies in the effort to achieve balance, for it is there that the churches must be in agreement. Failure to strive for balance in worship will ultimately cause the church's service of worship to fall short of the biblical ideal.[51]

If it is necessary to balance word and symbol, it is critical to balance Word and Sacrament. If there is anything that modern liturgical scholarship agrees on, it is that the Lord's Supper should be celebrated every Lord's Day as the church gathers to worship the risen Lord. We have seen Calvin's emphasis that true worship is worship involving both the Word and the Table. As von Allmen notes, the most basic reason that weekly communion is essential is that "Christ instituted it and commanded the Church to celebrate it."[52] Indeed, there is evidence that the New Testament church did just that.[53] The implications of apostolic practice, as well as the liturgical history of the church, indicate that weekly communion should be the norm and not the exception.

Theologically, there are some tremendous implications involved in the regular, weekly observance of the Lord's Supper. First, it is a sign of judgment, in that it discriminates those who have been admitted into the family from those who are yet without. Indeed, all who are admitted have undergone the waters of judgment in baptism and have been delivered.[54] Thus, there is an eschatological focus in that every time the communion is observed there is an anticipation of the final judgment when the people of God will be eternally separated from the unfaithful. Second, the Lord's Supper is an act of covenant bonding, with the sacramental tearing of the body and shedding of the blood of Jesus that enable the church to participate in his resurrection life.[55] Thus, we are reminded weekly that we already are participants in the life that is to come.

Third, the reenactment of the Last Supper is a remembrance by which the people of God participate sacramentally in the act of redemption on the cross, even as the Passover memorial united the Jews with the redemption of the exodus.[56] Through this action, the people of God have confirmed every Lord's Day the promise of forgiveness of sins. By reenacting these tremendous concepts every Lord's Day, the service of Word and Table provides a completely adequate response to God's initiatives. Moreover, the Lord's Supper is a response that satisfies nonrational human needs in worship even as it addresses the senses and the heart.

Must a church adopt weekly communion to be a Christian church? The legacy of the Reformation and historic Presbyterian practice tell us, of course, that this is not so. The better question would be, Do churches that practice infrequent communion miss out on benefits, personal and corporate, by failing to balance properly the emphasis on Word and Sacrament? For this there can be only one answer.

A radical change in Presbyterian thinking will not come easily, nor will it come quickly. However, if the Presbyterian churches are to be truly Reformed, they must not be satisfied with inherited practices that do not adequately represent the intentions of Scripture. Instead, they must make those first steps toward restoring the Lord's Supper to its rightful place as the normal worship of the church.

WORSHIP THAT IS CHRIST-CENTERED

The last, but arguably the most important, guideline is that worship must be Christ-centered. This should not be understood as somehow inimical to trinitarian worship.[57] On the contrary, all true worship is trinitarian in that it is for the glory of the Father, through the mediation of the Son, and in the power of the Holy Spirit. Further, it would be a serious christological error to understand a christocentric focus as somehow detracting from trinitarian worship.[58] Instead, the christocentric focus we are speaking of here carries with it several positive ideas that must inform the worship of the church.

First, all true worship centers on the person and work of Jesus Christ. The Christ event, then, is the all-controlling category of Christian worship. Every time the church gathers to worship, "there is a summing up of those events in history that constitute the source of the church's salvation. In worship we rehearse the gospel story. We rehearse, as it were, the Creation, Fall, Incarnation, Death, Resurrection, and Consummation. Therefore, our worship proclaims Jesus Christ and His saving reality again and again."[59] Significantly, it is in worship that the church experiences most pointedly the tension between this age and the eschaton. As von Allmen describes it, "The Christian cult, because it is based on the reconciliation of all things in Christ, is the advance-guard of that cosmic quest of which St. Paul speaks, that cosmic longing for a restitution of what God, in His love, had established at the first (Rom. 8:18ff)."[60]

Every gathering of the people of God to recapitulate the Christ event through the Word and the Table is, through the work of the Holy Spirit, a reenactment[61] of the work on the cross and an anticipation of the second advent.[62] T. F. Torrance reminds us that while the cross is a once-for-all event, there is a sacramental "re-living" of salvation through the power of the Holy Spirit through whom we "are so intimately united to Christ, by communion in his body and blood, that we participate in his self-consecration and self-offering to the Father."[63] Thus, "at every Eucharist, those who participate learn that they are themselves the objects of the redemptive action of the cross."[64] Likewise, the proclamation of the coming kingdom, as well as the symbolism of the eschatological banquet in the Lord's Supper, points the church forward to the greater realization of all the benefits now enjoyed by way of anticipation.

Second, all true worship is mediated through the work of Jesus Christ. This may be viewed from different perspectives. To begin with, Jesus Christ offers worship to the Father on behalf of the church. Thus, all worship is made acceptable to the Father because it is mediated through the Son as High Priest for the people of God. Jesus Christ, who clothed himself with humanity in order that he might offer up himself on behalf of his people, also ever lives to intercede on behalf of the church, sanctifying her worship and offering it to the Father as his own.[65] From another perspective, mediation involves the union that is sustained between Christ and his people, particularly in regard to worship. Torrance explains this in relation to the Lord's Supper:

> The eucharistic sacrifice means that we *through the Spirit* are so intimately united to Christ, by communion in his body and blood, that we participate in his self-consecration and self-offering to the Father and thus appear with him and in him and through him before the Majesty of God in worship, praise and adoration with no other sacrifice than the sacrifice of Christ Jesus our Mediator and High Priest. Conversely, the eucharistic sacrifice is the self-consecration and self-offering of Jesus Christ in our nature ascending to the Father from the Church in which he dwells through the Spirit he has poured out upon it, uniting it to himself as his Body, so that when the Church worships, praises and adores the Father through Christ and celebrates the Eucharist in his name, it is Christ himself who worships, praises and adores the Father in and through his members, taking up, moulding and sanctifying the prayers of his people as they are united to him through communion in his body and blood.[66]

Thus, Jesus Christ not only unites himself with the church in its worship, but is himself the content of the church's worship. If according to his human nature he lifts up the worship of the church unto the Father, according to his divine nature he is himself the focus of worship.[67]

Third, Jesus Christ is the ultimate parameter of worship. That is, Jesus, through his Spirit, teaches the church and leads the people of God into the fullness of worship. Poythress has commented on this in regard to a particular aspect of the church's worship, praise in song, that "Christ sings in us to write the law on our hearts (Heb. 8:10). This is part of the *application* of redemption and the application of Scripture."[68] Now, much could be said about the role of the Spirit in gifting the church with the *charismata* and leading the church in power. Suffice it to say here that the church must ever be open to the lordship of Jesus Christ, working through men and women gifted by his Spirit, to lead the church into new and greater understanding of his will.

Of course, there are dangers inherent in speaking of being led by Christ's Spirit. The one danger is to fail continually to relate the leading of the Spirit to the teaching of the Word. The other is so to fear the workings of the Spirit as to effectively eliminate his leading.[69] Both possibilities of error exist, but neither should intimidate the church into ignoring this greatest source of power and direction.

SUMMARY

In agreement with the biblical and historical findings of earlier chapters, we have attempted to establish a firm theological basis for the regulation of Christian worship. Our investigation has shown that worship, far from being esoteric in nature, is at bottom one with faithful service to God. Such service is not regulated by an endless number of rules governing every possible course of action. Rather, God has established his covenant with his people, and grounded their obedience in responsible conformity to his marvelous Word. Wisdom, gained from mature reflection on God, his Word, and the world around us, replaces reliance on an endless pedantic code of rules and regulations. Furthermore, the church has substantial freedom in many matters neither commanded nor prohibited. These may be used as the church wisely sees fit.

The people of God, however, are not freed from an extensive set of rules in order to act arbitrarily in their worship of the Lord. Rather, they are commanded to image God's own character by applying the parameters of covenantal regulation to their public, corporate acts of worship. As the Presbyterian churches contextualize the covenantal principle of worship, worship styles as diverse as those found in New Life churches and High Church settings will be validated. The covenantal principle of worship, applied to varying contexts and needs, will result not in sterile uniformity, but rather in a rich diversity of praise offered up to the glory of God.

CONCLUSION

At the beginning of this study, Presbyterian worship was described as confused due to the lack of consensus regarding foundational liturgical principles. Indeed, this problem is real. The answer, however, is not to repristinate the past. The notion that some past era was the golden age of liturgical faithfulness falls apart in light of the cold, hard reality of history. So efforts to return to the Geneva of the sixteenth century, or to the Scotland of the seventeenth century, are not the real answers to our difficulties. Instead, the answer lies in the genius of Reformed liturgy: the church's faithful application of abiding truths to the changing situations of the day.

So we return once more to the liturgical confusion that surrounds us. Our study has provided evidence that this description of the situation is fundamentally correct. And there are reasons for that confusion. We have seen that the Puritan regulative principle of worship was an exaggeration of, and departure from, the worship practice of John Calvin, whom the Puritans regarded as a leading father in the faith. We have also seen that the Puritan regulative principle of worship has been fraught with difficulties from the very beginning. Further consideration of biblical and theological principles has established beyond any reasonable doubt that the Puritan regulative principle exceeded the bounds established in

Scripture and imposed strictures on its adherents that were unduly narrow.

To criticize the Puritans, particularly their concepts of regulating worship, is not to indict Puritanism as a movement. As a whole, Puritanism exhibited remarkable fidelity to the Word of God. Even the immoderate pursuit of plainness may be attributed more to excessive zeal than to any other cause. Most importantly, the Puritans' continual witness to the importance of Scripture as determining the biblical basis for worship has provided Presbyterianism with a solid, if at times inconsistent, defense against liturgical trendiness and experimentation.

Today, however, we are in a new era. Developments in historical, biblical, and liturgical studies have provided new insights into the dynamics that gave birth to the Puritan regulative principle. Today we are able to separate those elements of Puritan thought that were culturally and polemically conditioned from those which reflected the truth of God's Word. Thus, on the basis of the best of Puritan thinking, along with certain key ideas represented by their Anglican opponents, we are able to forge a new direction in worship. With the insights provided from many diverse sources, we are able to structure a basis for worship that is faithful to the biblical commands, as well as consistent with biblical examples. By reaffirming the role of *adiaphora* in the church, we are able to replace the deficiencies of the Puritan formulation by the healthy tensions of covenant responsibility and creativity.

In essence, the covenantal principle of worship is not precisely a contradiction of the Puritan principle. Rather, it is organically related to it, stemming from the same desire to honor God that so permeated Puritan thought and practice. Moreover, there is a sense in which the covenantal principle, rooted firmly in Calvin's own thought, goes full circle, returning the wheel to its starting point. Based on the Puritan affirmation that God alone is sovereign in all matters, the covenantal principle seeks to integrate more successfully the responsibility of believers, as God's vicegerents, to engage in meaningful, faithful, biblical worship.

To the extent that we have built upon the Puritan foundation, modern Presbyterianism owes a great debt to the Puritan fathers. But, to the extent that the covenantal principle of worship is an advance over the Puritan principle, modern Presbyterianism owes an obligation to the Scriptures, to the Reformation, and most importantly, to the Lord of the church, who leads and guides its worship, to commit its efforts to liturgical renewal according to the boundaries of the Word. Therefore, modern Presbyterian worship must end the pursuit of plainness, and begin the pursuit of covenant faithfulness.

NOTES

INTRODUCTION: THE LONG AND WINDING ROAD

1. Terry L. Johnson, ed., *Leading in Worship* (Oak Ridge, Tenn.: Covenant Foundation, 1996), 1.
2. Wallace Radcliffe, "The Westminster Assembly, the Men and Their Work," in *Addresses at the Celebration of the Two Hundred and Fiftieth Anniversary of the Westminster Assembly by the General Assembly of the Presbyterian Church in the U.S.A.*, ed. William Henry Roberts (Philadelphia: Presbyterian Board of Publication and Sabbath-School Work, 1898), 154–55.
3. Will-worship is a term used by proponents of the Puritan regulative principle of worship to refer to any element of worship instituted by human will, not commanded by divine will in Scripture. See Westminster Confession of Faith, 21.1.
4. Originally, I was interested in a comparative study of John Cardinal Newman and William Cunningham, particularly with regard to their respective views on the development of doctrine.
5. See Adherents Website at http://www.adherents.com. Current figures are relatively in line with those I examined twelve years ago.
6. Adding the reported communicant members of the Reformed Presbyterian Church of North America (RPCNA), Associate Reformed Presbyterian Church (ARP), Orthodox Presbyterian Church (OPC), Evangelical Presbyterian Church (EPC), and Presbyterian Church in America (PCA) gives a combined figure of about 400,000.

CHAPTER 1: DOING YOUR OWN THING

1. Frank J. Smith, "What Is Worship?" in *Worship in the Presence of God*, ed. Frank J. Smith and David C. Lachman (Greenville, S.C.: Greenville Seminary Press, 1992), 16–17.

2. John M. Frame, *Worship in Spirit and Truth* (Phillipsburg, N.J.: Presbyterian and Reformed, 1996), xiii.

3. Technically, the principle *lex orandi, lex credendi* argues that the practice of prayer underlies and precedes belief and action. Thus, piety may express itself genuinely in spite of serious theoretical flaws in one's theology. For a definition, see Richard A. Muller, *Dictionary of Latin and Greek Theological Terms* (Grand Rapids: Baker, 1985), 175.

4. Many congregations have embraced "blended worship," which is a convergence of ancient and contemporary practices. See Robert Webber, *Blended Worship* (Peabody, Mass.: Hendrickson, 1996).

5. The mainline Presbyterian Church (USA) has taken liturgical renewal far more seriously than have evangelical Presbyterians. They have produced two worship books since 1970: *The Worshipbook: Services* (Philadelphia: Westminster, 1970); and *The Book of Common Worship* (Louisville: Westminster/John Knox, 1993).

6. Ray Stedman, *Body Life* (Ventura, Calif.: Regal, 1972).

7. Robert A. Morey, *Worship Is All of Life* (Camp Hill, Pa.: Christian Publications, 1984).

8. Robert Webber, "Enter His Courts with Praise," *Reformed Worship* 20 (June 1991): 9–12.

9. Robert Webber, *Evangelicals on the Canterbury Trail* (Waco: Jarrell, 1985), 15. See also *Common Roots: A Call to Evangelical Maturity* (Grand Rapids: Zondervan, 1978), and *Worship Old and New* (Grand Rapids: Zondervan, 1982).

10. Robert Webber, *Worship Is a Verb* (Waco: Word, 1985).

11. Thomas Howard, *Evangelical Is Not Enough* (Nashville: Thomas Nelson, 1984), 149.

12. Ibid., 109. After publishing this volume, Howard converted to Roman Catholicism.

13. *The Complete Library of Christian Worship*, ed. Robert Webber, 8 vols. (Nashville: Star Song, 1993–94). In more recent volumes, Webber has begun to call for evangelicals to embrace convergence worship that blends both High Church and Low Church elements.

14. Anne Ortlund, *Up with Worship* (Ventura, Calif.: Regal, 1975).

15. Robert G. Rayburn, *O Come, Let Us Worship* (Grand Rapids: Baker, 1980).

16. Ralph P. Martin, *The Worship of God* (Grand Rapids: Eerdmans, 1982).

17. Warren W. Wiersbe, *Real Worship* (Nashville: Oliver Nelson, 1986); and Ronald Allen and Gordon Borror, *Worship: Rediscovering the Missing Jewel* (Portland, Ore.: Multnomah, 1982). Conspicuously and inexplicably absent from both volumes is any emphasis on the importance of frequent communion in worship. This emphasis is a hallmark of modern liturgical scholarship, and it is unfortunate when it is ignored in a text on worship.

18. "Worship," *Leadership* 7.2 (spring 1986).
19. Jack Miller was also largely responsible for the "Sonship" movement within Presbyterian churches.
20. See, for example, George Miladin, "Hymns Don't Need to Be Vertical," *Presbyterian Journal*, 23 May 1984, 10–11.
21. Bernard J. Stonehouse, "Worship Regulated by the Scriptures," *Presbyterian Journal*, 4 February 1987, 13.
22. James B. Jordan, *The Sociology of the Church* (Tyler, Tex.: Geneva Ministries, 1986). See also James B. Jordan, ed., *The Reconstruction of the Church*, vol. 4 in *Christianity and Civilization* (Tyler, Tex.: Geneva Ministries, 1985).
23. Jordan, *Sociology of the Church*, 31.
24. Representative works expounding traditional Presbyterian practice, as determined by the principles exemplified in the Westminster Assembly's Directory for the Publick Worship of God (found in *Westminster Confession of Faith* [1646; reprint, Glasgow: Free Presbyterian Publications, 1976], 369–94), are the following: (1) the symposium, *The Biblical Doctrine of Worship* (n.p.: Committee on Worship: Reformed Presbyterian Church of North America, 1974); (2) the study guide on worship, Paul E. Engle, *Discovering the Fullness of Worship* (Philadelphia: Great Commission Publications, 1978); and (3) the recent work by Smith and Lachman, *Worship in the Presence of God*.
25. A volume from within the Christian Reformed Church is worthy of notice, maintaining as it does the less stringent continental approach to the regulation of worship. See James A. De Jong, *Into His Presence* (Grand Rapids: Board of Publications of the Christian Reformed Church, 1985). Another CRC publication worthy of note is the quarterly *Reformed Worship*. Also in the continental tradition is the small but helpful volume by G. Vandooren, *The Beauty of Reformed Liturgy* (Winnipeg: Premier Publishing, 1980).
26. Paul Waitman Hoon, *The Integrity of Worship* (Nashville: Abingdon, 1971), 10.
27. Ibid.

CHAPTER 2: DÉJÀ VU ALL OVER AGAIN

1. For that reason, the term "Puritan regulative principle of worship" will be used in this study to designate this concept in its historical and confessional fullness.
2. James F. White, *Protestant Worship* (Louisville: Westminster/John Knox, 1989), 23.
3. James F. White, "Where the Reformation Was Wrong on Worship," *Christian Century*, 27 October 1962, 1075.
4. Ibid., 1076.

5. Benjamin B. Warfield, *The Westminster Assembly and Its Work*, vol. 6 in *The Works of Benjamin B. Warfield* (1931; reprint, Grand Rapids: Baker, 1981), 45.

6. The Shorter Catechism makes no significant contribution to the discussion at hand.

7. Of course, there is a clear parallel between a *jus divinum* or "divine law" view of Presbyterianism and the regulative principle of worship; nevertheless, such considerations are beyond the scope of this work.

8. The text is from the critical edition prepared by S. W. Carruthers, *The Westminster Confession of Faith* (Manchester: R. Aikman and Son, n.d.). All other WCF references will be from this edition and will be referenced only by chapter and section.

9. John Murray, "The Importance and Relevance of the Westminster Confession," in *The Claims of Truth*, vol. 1 in *Collected Writings of John Murray* (Carlisle, Pa.: Banner of Truth, 1976), 317.

10. A. A. Hodge, *The Confession of Faith* (1869; reprint, Carlisle, Pa.: Banner of Truth, 1978), 37.

11. G. I. Williamson, *The Westminster Confession of Faith for Study Classes* (Philadelphia: Presbyterian and Reformed, 1964), 11.

12. James Bannerman, *The Church of Christ*, 2 vols. (1869; reprint, Carlisle, Pa.: Banner of Truth, 1974), 1:340.

13. The Lutheran principle of worship is virtually identical to the Anglican principle. James Moffatt, "Luther," in *Christian Worship*, ed. Nathaniel Micklem (London: Oxford University Press, 1936), 125, notes that "unless an existing form of worship was plainly inconsistent with the Word of the gospel, there was no obligation to surrender it." For the Lutheran confessional statement, see the Formula of Concord, Article 10, "Of Church Rites," in Philip Schaff, *The Creeds of Christendom*, 6th ed., 3 vols., revised by David S. Schaff (1931; reprint, Grand Rapids: Baker, 1983), 3:160–64.

14. This is the 1571 English text as found in Schaff, *Creeds*, 3:500.

15. George Gillespie, *A Treatise of Miscellany Questions*, in vol. 2 of *The Presbyterian's Armoury*, 3 vols. (1649; reprint, Edinburgh: Robert Ogle and Oliver and Boyd, 1846), 83.

16. Samuel Rutherford, *Lex, Rex, or The Law and the Prince* (1644; reprint, Harrisonburg, Va.: Sprinkle, 1982), 83–84. See also 214, 217.

17. John Owen, *Church Purity and Unity*, vol. 15 in *The Works of John Owen*, ed. William H. Goold (1850–53 edition; reprint, Carlisle, Pa.: Banner of Truth, 1965), 40.

18. *The Larger Catechism* (1648; reprint, n.p.: Free Presbyterian Publications, 1981), 193–96.

19. Gillespie, *Treatise of Miscellany Questions*, 83, says that circumstances are "so numerous and so various that all circumstances belonging to all times and places could not be particularly determined in Scriptures, yet the

church ought to order them so, and hath power to order them otherwise, as may best agree with the general rules of the word."

20. Hodge, *Confession of Faith*, 39.
21. Williamson, *Westminster Confession of Faith for Study Classes*, 11.
22. Robert Shaw, *An Exposition of the Confession of Faith* (Philadelphia: Presbyterian Board of Publication, 1846), 28.
23. Edmund Clowney, "Distinctive Emphases in Presbyterian Church Polity," in *Pressing toward the Mark*, ed. Charles G. Dennison and Richard C. Gamble Jr. (Philadelphia: Committee for the Historian of the OPC, 1986), 101.
24. John L. Girardeau, *Instrumental Music in Church Worship* (1888; reprint, Havertown, Pa.: New Covenant Publication Society, n.d.), 188–99.
25. The great Hodge-Thornwell debate on the nature of Presbyterian church government vis-à-vis church boards and *jure divino* Presbyterianism was over the application of the regulative principle in the matter of church polity. The whole controversy, which ended but was not resolved, turned on the nature and meaning of "circumstances." See James Henley Thornwell, *The Collected Works of James Henry Thornwell*, vol. 4, *Ecclesiastical*, ed. B. M. Palmer (1875; reprint, Carlisle, Pa.: Banner of Truth, 1974), 143–296; see the appendix (p. 616) for Charles Hodge's opposing article "Presbyterianism." For a summary of this issue, see Clowney, "Distinctive Emphases in Presbyterian Church Polity," 110.
26. Helpful summaries of Gillespie's position may be found in either James Bannerman, *Church of Christ*, 1:355–57; or Iain Murray, "Scripture and 'Things Indifferent,'" in *Diversity in Unity*, papers read at the Puritan and Reformed Studies Conference, London, Dec. 1963, pp. 26–27.
27. George Gillespie, *A Dispute against the English Popish Ceremonies*, in vol. 1 of *The Presbyterian's Armoury*, 3 vols. (1660; reprint, Edinburgh: Robert Ogle and Oliver and Boyd, 1846), 130.
28. See Bannerman, *Church of Christ*, 1:355.
29. Gillespie, *Dispute against the English Popish Ceremonies*, 132.
30. Ibid., 133.
31. Bannerman, *Church of Christ*, 1:357. John Owen, *Church Purity and Unity*, 35, offers helpful insight: "Circumstances are either such as follow actions as actions, or such as are arbitrarily superadded and adjoined by command unto actions, which do not of their own accord, nor naturally nor necessarily attend them."
32. Owen, *Church Purity and Unity*, 35.
33. William Cunningham, *The Reformers and the Theology of the Reformation* (1862; reprint, Carlisle, Pa.: Banner of Truth, 1979), 32.
34. Hodge, *Confession of Faith*, 265.
35. Williamson, *Westminster Confession of Faith for Study Classes*, 150.
36. Hodge, *Confession of Faith*, 265.

37. *Adiaphora* are things neither commanded nor forbidden.
38. Carruthers, *Westminster Confession of Faith,* 128.
39. George S. Hendry, *The Westminster Confession for Today* (Atlanta: John Knox, 1960), 183.
40. Robert Baillie, one of the Scots commissioners, notes with some aggravation that prior to the Westminster Assembly, the Scottish Kirk had been divided over the issue of "novations," or the practice of some more extreme ministers to leave off the historic Scottish practices of using the Lord's Prayer, the Gloria, and kneeling in the pulpit. The General Assembly attempted to tread a middle path, recognizing the "innocence" of these practices while trying to keep peace in the church by not imposing their use. See Robert Baillie, *The Letters and Journals of Robert Baillie,* ed. David Laing, 3 vols. (reprint, Edinburgh: Robert Ogle, 1841), 2:51, 69–70.
41. Gillespie, *Dispute against the English Popish Ceremonies,* 58–109, attacks Anglican practices from virtually every angle possible, to demonstrate that they, since not required by Scripture, are in essence idolatrous.
42. Hodge, *Confession of Faith,* 271.
43. Williamson, *Westminster Confession of Faith for Study Classes,* 159.
44. Ibid.
45. Bannerman, *Church of Christ,* 1:352.
46. *The Form of Presbyterial Church Government* (1646; reprint, Glasgow: Free Presbyterian Publications, 1976), 404.
47. Robert F. Coyle, "The Westminster Polity and Worship," in *Addresses at the Celebration of the Two Hundred and Fiftieth Anniversary of the Westminster Assembly by the General Assembly of the Presbyterian Church in the U.S.A.,* ed. William Henry Roberts (Philadelphia: Presbyterian Board of Publication and Sabbath-School Work, 1898), 132.
48. The Savoy Declaration differs only in details from the Westminster Confession of Faith, being altered to suit Independent Puritans. It does appear to strengthen the chapter on "Christian Liberty"; see Schaff, *Creeds,* 3:707–29, especially p. 719.
49. Robert L. Dabney, *Discussions of Robert Lewis Dabney,* 3 vols. (1891–97; reprint, Carlisle, Pa.: Banner of Truth, 1982), 2:97; William Cunningham, *Reformers and the Theology of the Reformation,* 32–37, "the principle"; and James Bannerman, *Church of Christ,* 2:345, "principles of truth," "principles of order which enable it to regulate," and 2:359, "rule for regulating."
50. George Hays, *Presbyterians* (New York: J. A. Hill and Co., 1892), 413–24; and R. J. George, *Lectures in Pastoral Theology* (New York: Christian Nation, 1917).
51. Julius Melton, *Presbyterian Worship in America* (Richmond: John Knox, 1967), 30.
52. Samuel Miller, "The Worship of the Presbyterian Church," in *Presbyterian Tracts,* vol. 10 (Philadelphia: Presbyterian Board of Publication, n.d.), #197, 1.

53. Ibid., 2.
54. Bannerman, *Church of Christ*, 2:340.
55. Cunningham, *Reformers and the Theology of the Reformation*, 31–32.
56. Ibid., 33.
57. Dabney, *Discussions of Robert Lewis Dabney*, 1:501–2.
58. Robert L. Dabney, *Lectures in Systematic Theology* (1878; reprint, Grand Rapids: Zondervan, 1976), 361.

CHAPTER 3: THE PURITAN VIA MEDIA

1. Benjamin B. Warfield, *The Westminster Assembly and Its Work*, vol. 6 in *The Works of Benjamin B. Warfield* (1931; reprint, Grand Rapids: Baker, 1981), 45.
2. Alexander F. Mitchell, *The Westminster Assembly—Its History and Standards* (Philadelphia: Presbyterian Board of Publication, 1884), 214–15.
3. Horton Davies, *The Worship of the English Puritans* (Westminster: Dacre, 1948), examines Puritan worship in great detail.
4. See Alexander F. Mitchell, *Minutes of the Sessions of the Westminster Assembly of Divines* (Edinburgh: William Blackwood and Sons, 1874), 356, 484.
5. Directory for the Publick Worship of God, in *Westminster Confession of Faith* (1646; reprint, Glasgow: Free Presbyterian Publications, 1976), 373.
6. Ibid., 374.
7. Ibid.
8. Ibid., 387–88.
9. Ibid., 393–94.
10. Ibid., 386.
11. Robert F. Coyle, "The Westminster Polity and Worship," in *Addresses at the Celebration of the Two Hundred and Fiftieth Anniversary of the Westminster Assembly by the General Assembly of the Presbyterian Church in the U.S.A.*, ed. William Henry Roberts (Philadelphia: Presbyterian Board of Publication and Sabbath-School Work, 1898), 154; Warfield, *Westminster Assembly and Its Work*, 46; Mitchell, *Westminster Assembly—Its History and Standards*, 231–37.
12. "A directory, as opposed to a liturgy." Bard Thompson, *Liturgies of the Western Church* (Philadelphia: Fortress, 1961), 349.
13. Coyle, "Westminster Polity and Worship," 154.
14. Mitchell, *Westminster Assembly—Its History and Standards*, 221.
15. Robert Baillie, *The Letters and Journals of Robert Baillie*, ed. David Laing, 3 vols. (reprint, Edinburgh: Robert Ogle, 1841), 2:242.
16. Directory for the Publick Worship of God, 374.
17. Ibid., 379.

18. Ibid., 382.
19. That is, innovations.
20. Warfield, *Westminster Assembly and Its Work*, 47.
21. Davies, *Worship of the English Puritans*, 133; Gillespie's list of unacceptable matters included some items objectionable to the English and others objectionable to the Scots. George Gillespie, *Notes of Debates and Proceedings of the Assembly of Divines*, in vol. 2 of *The Presbyterian's Armoury* (Edinburgh: Robert Ogle and Oliver and Boyd, 1846), 108. It was agreed to omit this list from the Directory (p. 97).
22. John Lightfoot, *The Whole Works of the Rev. John Lightfoot, D.D.*, vol. 13, *The Journal of the Proceedings of the Assembly of Divines* (London: J. F. Dove, 1824), 286–96.
23. Baillie, *Letters and Journals of Robert Baillie*, 2:148, described their practice as "very irreverent." See also Gillespie, *Notes of Debates and Proceedings of the Assembly of Divines*, 102.
24. Baillie, *Letters and Journals of Robert Baillie*, 2:187.
25. Thomas Leishman, *The Westminster Directory* (Edinburgh: William Blackwood and Sons, 1901), 114–34.
26. Lightfoot, *Journal of the Proceedings of the Assembly of Divines*, 340.
27. Davies, *Worship of the English Puritans*, 138.
28. Lightfoot, *Journal of the Proceedings of the Assembly of Divines*, 284.
29. Ibid., 91–92.
30. Mitchell, *Westminster Assembly—Its History and Standards*, 221.
31. Interestingly, both Leishman, *Westminster Directory*, xxiv, and Robert S. Paul, *The Assembly of the Lord* (Edinburgh: T. and T. Clark, 1985), 315, refer to the decreasing influence of the Scots in the Westminster Assembly as time went on.
32. Coyle, "Westminster Polity and Worship," 155.
33. Mitchell, *Westminster Assembly—Its History and Standards*, 232, notes the solicitous efforts on the part of the assembly to assure acceptance by the Scots.
34. Ibid., 231.

CHAPTER 4: REGULATING WITH CALVIN

1. John Calvin, *Institutes of the Christian Religion*, 1536 edition, trans. Ford Lewis Battles (Grand Rapids: Eerdmans, 1975); and John Calvin, *Institutes of the Christian Religion*, 1559 edition, ed. John T. McNeill, trans. Ford Lewis Battles, Library of Christian Classics, vols. 20–21 (Philadelphia: Westminster, 1960).
2. Ronald S. Wallace, *Calvin's Doctrine of the Word and Sacrament* (1953; reprint, Tyler, Tex.: Geneva Divinity School Press, 1982), 96–97.

3. W. Robert Godfrey, "Biblical Authority in the Sixteenth and Seventeenth Centuries: A Question of Transition," in *Scripture and Truth*, ed. D. A. Carson and John D. Woodbridge (Grand Rapids: Zondervan, 1983), 234.

4. John Calvin, *Commentaries on the Epistles to Timothy, Titus, and Philemon*, trans. William Pringle (reprint, Grand Rapids: Baker, 1982), commenting on 2 Timothy 3:16–17.

5. John Calvin, *Sermons on the Ten Commandments*, trans. and ed. Benjamin W. Farley (Grand Rapids: Baker, 1980), 66.

6. Thomas F. Torrance, *Calvin's Doctrine of Man* (1957; reprint, Westport, Conn.: Greenwood, 1977), 115.

7. Calvin, *Sermons on the Ten Commandments*, 66.

8. John Calvin, *Sermons on Deuteronomy*, trans. Arthur Golding (1583; reprint, Carlisle, Pa.: Banner of Truth, 1987), 149.

9. Ibid., 463.

10. Carlos M. N. Eire, *War against the Idols* (Cambridge: Cambridge University Press, 1986), 201–2.

11. Wilhelm Pauck, "Calvin's Institutes of the Christian Religion," *Church History* 15 (1946): 19.

12. Benjamin Charles Milner, *Calvin's Doctrine of the Church*, vol. 5 in *Studies in the History of Christian Thought*, ed. Heiko Oberman (Leiden: E. J. Brill, 1970), 158. See also John Calvin, *Commentary on the Book of Psalms*, trans. James Anderson (1845; reprint, Grand Rapids: Baker, 1981), commenting on Psalm 100:4.

13. John Calvin, *Commentaries on the Twelve Minor Prophets*, trans. John Owen (1848; reprint, Grand Rapids: Baker, 1982), 4:368–69.

14. H. W. Rossouw, "Calvin's Hermeneutics of Holy Scripture," in *Calvinus Reformator* (Potchefstroom: Potchefstroom University for Higher Christian Education, 1982), 152.

15. Richard A. Muller, *Dictionary of Latin and Greek Theological Terms* (Grand Rapids: Baker, 1985), 33.

16. Thomas F. Torrance, *The Hermeneutics of John Calvin* (Edinburgh: Scottish Academic Press, 1988), 50–57, 87–95. He discusses John Major's contribution to Calvin's interpretation of Scripture and his understanding of "the nature of theological statement" (p. 90). Torrance suggests, among other influences, that Major's interest in "statements" and not words alone, context and not mere signification, is an important factor in Calvin's hermeneutics (p. 54).

17. Rossouw, "Calvin's Hermeneutics," 180. Willem Balke, *Calvin and the Anabaptist Radicals*, trans. William J. Heynen (Grand Rapids: Eerdmans, 1981), 326–27, also notes Calvin's complaint about the Anabaptist tendency toward biblicism.

18. Ford Lewis Battles, *Interpreting John Calvin*, ed. Robert Benedetto (Grand Rapids: Baker, 1996), 299.
19. Donald K. McKim, "Calvin's View of Scripture," in *Readings in Calvin's Theology*, ed. Donald K. McKim (Grand Rapids: Baker, 1984), 49.
20. Bernard Zylstra, "Thy Word Our Life," in *Will All the King's Men*, ed. James H. Olthuis et al. (Toronto: Wedge, 1972), 183–84.
21. John Calvin, *Treatises against the Anabaptists and against the Libertines*, ed. and trans. Benjamin W. Farley (Grand Rapids: Baker, 1982), 30.
22. Curiously, it is just this interest in harmonizing exegesis that H. Jackson Forstman, *Word and Spirit* (Stanford: Stanford University Press, 1962), 123, criticizes, noting that any attempt to harmonize the teaching of Scripture is hopeless. However, Rossouw, "Calvin's Hermeneutics," 176, finds this an essential and valuable element of Calvin as interpreter, namely, his efforts at harmonizing the biblical data.
23. Thomas Watson Street, "John Calvin on *Adiaphora*: An Exposition and Appraisal of His Theory and Practice," Th.D. diss., Union Theological Seminary, 1954, vi–vii.
24. Ibid., 65.
25. Wilhelm Niesel, *The Theology of Calvin*, trans. Harold Knight (1956; reprint, Grand Rapids: Baker, 1980), 99–100.
26. Street, "John Calvin on *Adiaphora*," 69.
27. Ronald S. Wallace, *Calvin's Doctrine of the Christian Life* (1959; reprint, Tyler, Tex.: Geneva Divinity School Press, 1982), 311.
28. See *ICR*, 3.19.2–13; also, Street, "John Calvin on *Adiaphora*," 75.
29. John Calvin, *Commentary on the Epistles of Paul the Apostle to the Corinthians*, trans. John Pringle (1848; reprint, Grand Rapids: Baker, 1981), 214.
30. "Conscience" is his focal point in both 3.19 and 4.10. See Street, "John Calvin on *Adiaphora*," 116.
31. Ibid., 117–18.
32. John Calvin, *Commentaries on the Epistles of Paul the Apostle to the Philippians, Colossians, and Thessalonians*, trans. John Pringle (1851; reprint, Grand Rapids: Baker, 1981), 193; see comment on Col. 2:17.
33. John Calvin, *Commentary upon the Acts of the Apostles*, trans. Christopher Fetherstone, ed. Henry Beveridge (reprint, Grand Rapids: Baker, 1981), 2:52, comment on Acts 15:10.
34. John Calvin, *Commentaries on the Four Last Books of Moses Arranged in the Form of a Harmony*, trans. Charles William Bingham (1852; reprint, Grand Rapids: Baker, 1982), 2:111, comment on Deut. 5:9.
35. Calvin, *Sermons on Deuteronomy*, 58.
36. In terms of Westminster's distinction, these are all "circumstances."
37. Street, "John Calvin on *Adiaphora*," 121.

CHAPTER 5: WORSHIP, GENEVAN STYLE

1. Ronald S. Wallace, *Calvin's Doctrine of the Word and Sacrament* (1953; reprint, Tyler, Tex.: Geneva Divinity School Press, 1982), 243.
2. Howard G. Hageman, *Pulpit and Table* (Richmond: John Knox, 1962), 17.
3. *The New Westminster Dictionary of Liturgy and Worship*, s.v. "bidding prayer."
4. See especially J. S. Whale, "Calvin," in *Christian Worship*, ed. Nathaniel Micklem (London: Oxford University Press, 1936), 170–71.
5. William D. Maxwell, *A History of Christian Worship* (1936; reprint, Grand Rapids: Baker, 1982), 116.
6. See also "Articles concerning the Organization of the Church and of Worship at Geneva Proposed by the Ministers at the Council, January 16, 1537," in *Calvin: Theological Treatises*, ed. and trans. J. K. S. Reid, Library of Christian Classics, Ichthus edition (Philadelphia: Westminster, 1954), 49.
7. Bard Thompson, *Liturgies of the Western Church* (Philadelphia: Fortress, 1961), 194.
8. James B. Jordan, *The Sociology of the Church* (Tyler, Tex.: Genevan Ministries, 1986), 29; James Hastings Nichols, *Corporate Worship in the Reformed Tradition* (Philadelphia: Westminster, 1968), 19.
9. H. Jackson Forstman, *Word and Spirit* (Stanford: Stanford University Press, 1962), 25.
10. Hughes Oliphant Old, *Guides to the Reformed Tradition: Worship* (Atlanta: John Knox, 1984), 132–33. See also Wallace, *Calvin's Doctrine of the Word and Sacrament*, 240–41.
11. Thompson, *Liturgies of the Western Church*, 334.
12. "The Book of Discipline 1587," in *The Reformation of the Church*, ed. Iain H. Murray (1965; reprint, Carlisle, Pa.: Banner of Truth, 1987), 184.
13. The Directory for the Publick Worship of God, in *Westminster Confession of Faith* (1646; reprint, Glasgow: Free Presbyterian Publications, 1976), 384; also, Thompson, *Liturgies of the Western Church*, 351.
14. Thompson, *Liturgies of the Western Church*, 300, 291, respectively. See especially William McMillan, *The Worship of the Scottish Reformed Church, 1550–1638* (Dunfermline: Lassodie, 1931), 190–97, which provides citations from numerous records indicating that Scottish Presbyterian practice was often less than quarterly due to the lack of ministers and the development of the "communion season."
15. Horton Davies, *The Worship of the English Puritans* (Westminster: Dacre, 1948), 42–43.
16. An excellent historical survey of this controversy is found in Benjamin B. Warfield, "The Posture of the Recipients at the Lord's Supper," in *Selected Shorter Writings of Benjamin B. Warfield*, 2 vols., ed. John H. Meeter (Nutley, N.J.: Presbyterian and Reformed, 1973), 2:351–69.

17. In this period, kneeling was inconsistently enforced, although officially required. The Puritan objection went beyond opposition to the *imposition* of kneeling to kneeling *per se* as not commanded in the Word of God. See J. I. Packer, "The Puritan Approach to Worship," in *Diversity in Unity*, papers read at the Puritan and Reformed Studies Conference, London, Dec. 1963, p. 5.

18. *The Oxford Dictionary of the Christian Church*, 3d ed., s.v. "black rubric."

19. Hageman, *Pulpit and Table*, 29; Davies, *Worship of the English Puritans*, 37. Note that kneeling for prayer was encouraged by Calvin as well (*ICR*, 3.20.33).

20. "Of the Celebration of the Communion, or Sacrament of the Lord's Supper," in Directory for the Publick Worship of God, 385.

21. John M. Barkley, *The Worship of the Reformed Church* (London: Lutterworth, 1966), 27.

22. Referred to in a letter to Heinrich Bullinger, dated June 1538; John Calvin, *Selected Works of John Calvin: Tracts and Letters*, ed. Henry Beveridge and Jules Bonnet, 7 vols. (1858; reprint, Grand Rapids: Baker, 1983), 7:393.

23. Davies, *Worship of the English Puritans*, 37; Wilhelm Niesel, *The Theology of Calvin*, trans. Harold Knight (1956; reprint, Grand Rapids: Baker, 1980), 206–7.

24. Patrick Collinson, *The Elizabethan Puritan Movement* (Berkeley: University of California Press, 1967), 36; Davies, *Worship of the English Puritans*, 37.

25. Joseph Ketley, ed., *The Two Liturgies, A.D. 1549 and A.D. 1552*, Parker Society (Cambridge: University Press, 1844), 97.

26. Ibid., 283.

27. *Liturgical Services of the Reign of Queen Elizabeth*, ed. William Clay, Parker Society (Cambridge: University Press, 1847), 399.

28. "The Necessity for Reformation: The Admonition to the Parliament 1572," in *The Reformation of the Church*, ed. Iain Murray (1965; reprint, Carlisle, Pa.: Banner of Truth, 1987), 89.

29. Directory for the Publick Worship of God, 374.

30. The concept of a service book for congregational use was novel. Earlier practice involved the use of several volumes, in Latin, by the officiant. See Henry Barclay Swete, *Church Services and Service-Books before the Reformation* (London: S.P.C.K., 1896), 15–20, for a description of pre-Reformation practice.

31. Thompson, *Liturgies of the Western Church*, 194–95.

32. Calvin, *Selected Works*, 5:191–92.

33. These are given in outline form in Maxwell, *History of Christian Worship*, 114–15. The content of the services outlined by Maxwell is given in full in Thompson, *Liturgies of the Western Church*, 197–210.

34. Thompson, *Liturgies of the Western Church*, 191; Hageman, *Pulpit and Table*, 29.

35. W. Stanford Reid, "Knox's Attitude to the English Reformation," *Westminster Theological Journal* 26.1 (Nov. 1963): 24–27.
36. *The Register of the Company of Pastors of Geneva in the Time of Calvin*, ed. and trans. Philip E. Hughes (Grand Rapids: Eerdmans, 1966), 44, under the year 1541. Also, see page 55, under the year 1546, for further regulations on godparents.
37. William Maxwell, *The Liturgical Portions of the Genevan Service Book* (1931; reprint, Westminster: Faith, 1965), 114.
38. "Ordinances for Supervision of Churches in the Country," in *Calvin: Theological Treatises*, 79. The service of baptism, with the questions asked of the parents/godparents, is found in J. D. C. Fisher, *Christian Initiation: The Reformation Period* (London: S.P.C.K., 1970), 112–17. Knox's service of baptism may be found here as well (pp. 118–23).
39. Davies, *Worship of the English Puritans*, 217.
40. From the 1559 prayer book in *Liturgical Services of the Reign of Queen Elizabeth*, 205. See also the expectation that godparents will have successfully instructed their godchildren in preparation for their confirmation (p. 210).
41. Exceptions against the Book of Common Prayer, in *Documents Relating to the Settlement of the Church of England by the Act of Uniformity, 1662*, ed. George Gould (London: W. Kent and Co., 1862), 133. Yet, some room (albeit minimal) for godparents is made here.
42. "The same day certain ordinances were proposed concerning the reformation of the village parishes. These were found to be good and useful." From the preamble to the "Ordinances for Supervision of Churches in the Country," in *Calvin: Theological Treatises*, 76.
43. A. H. Drysdale, *History of the Presbyterians in England* (London: Publication Committee of the Presbyterian Church of England, 1889), 57.
44. Calvin, *Selected Works*, 5:307.
45. Davies, *Worship of the English Puritans*, 46–47; Maxwell, *Liturgical Portions of the Genevan Service Book*, 210–13.
46. Robert W. Oliver, "The Externals of Worship," in *Anglican and Puritan Thinking* (London: Westminster Conference, 1977), 69.
47. R. J. Bauckham, "Sabbath and Sunday in the Protestant Tradition," in *From Sabbath to Lord's Day*, ed. D. A. Carson (Grand Rapids: Zondervan, 1982), 316.
48. John Calvin, *Sermons on the Ten Commandments*, trans. and ed. Benjamin W. Farley (Grand Rapids: Baker, 1980), 101.
49. Ibid., 110. Consider Calvin's comments in the Catechism of the Church of Geneva that "the observation of rest is part of the old ceremonies [and] . . . was therefore by the advent of Christ abrogated." He points out the abiding spiritual significance of the Sabbath, namely, being grafted into Christ and ceasing from our own works, *Calvin: Theological Treatises*, 111–13. Con-

sider also the emphasis in the confessional tradition. For example, the Heidelberg Catechism (in Philip Schaff, *The Creeds of Christendom*, 6th ed., 3 vols., revised by David S. Schaff [1931; reprint, Grand Rapids: Baker, 1983], 3:345), Q. 103: "What does God require in the fourth commandment?" Answer: "In the first place, that the ministry of the Gospel and schools be maintained; and that I, especially on the day of rest, diligently attend church, to learn the Word of God, to use the Holy Sacraments, to call publicly upon the Lord, and to give Christian alms. In the second place, that all the days of my life *I rest from my evil works, allow the Lord to work in me by his Spirit, and thus begin in this life the everlasting Sabbath*" (emphasis mine). Compare this with chapter 24 of the Second Helvetic Confession (Schaff, *The Creeds of Christendom*, 3:899)!

50. Barkley, *Worship of the Reformed Church*, 28. Indeed, the continental attitude is exhibited further in the fact that the Synod of Dort, 1618–19, "adopted a church order that included the observance of various days on the Christian calendar (art. 67)" (Stephen Doe, "The Observance of Christmas," accessed April 14, 2001 at http://www.opc.org/new_horizons/Christmas_observance.html). Many Reformed churches in the Dutch tradition still have similar articles in their updated versions of the Church Order of Dort.

51. René Guerdan, *La Vie quotidienne à Genève au temps de Calvin* (Paris: Librairie Hachette, 1973), 169.

52. Daniel Neal, *The History of the Puritans*, 3 vols. (1837; reprint, Minneapolis: Klock and Klock, 1979), 1:157. No provision is made in Westminster's Directory for the Publick Worship of God for holy days (pp. 386, 392).

53. Davies, *Worship of the English Puritans*, 42.

54. Thomas Becon, *Prayers and Other Pieces of Thomas Becon, S.T.P.*, ed. John Ayre, Parker Society (Cambridge: University Press, 1844), 234. The Elizabethan rite of confirmation is found in *Liturgical Services of the Reign of Queen Elizabeth*, 214–16.

55. William Fulke, "A Brief and Plain Declaration," in Leonard J. Trinterud, *Elizabethan Puritanism* (New York: Oxford University Press, 1971), 271–72.

56. Edmund Calamy, "The Grounds of the Nonconformity of the Ministers Who Were Ejected," in *The Reformation of the Church*, ed. Iain Murray (1965; reprint, Carlisle, Pa.: Banner of Truth, 1987), 162.

57. Exceptions against the Book of Common Prayer, 133.

58. Barkley, *Worship of the Reformed Church*, 25.

59. Maxwell, *History of Christian Worship*, 114–15; W. J. B. Serfontein, "John Calvin and the Protestant Hymns," in *Calvinus Reformator* (Potchefstroom: Potchefstroom University for Higher Christian Education, 1982), 226.

60. Serfontein, "John Calvin and the Protestant Hymns," 229.

61. Davies, *Worship of the English Puritans*, 48.

62. Packer, "Puritan Approach to Worship," 4.
63. Iain Murray discusses extensively the narrow application of the Puritan view of *adiaphora* in "Scripture and 'Things Indifferent,'" in *Diversity in Unity*, papers read at the Puritan and Reformed Studies Conference, London, Dec. 1963, pp. 26–28.
64. William Ames, *The Marrow of Theology*, trans. and ed. from 3d Latin edition, 1629, by John D. Eusden (Durham, N.C.: Labyrinth, 1968), 280.
65. William Ames, *A Fresh Suit against Human Ceremonies in God's Worship* (1633; reprint, Gregg International, 1971), 171.
66. John Flavel, "Antipharmacum Saluberrimum," in *The Works of John Flavel*, 6 vols. (1820; reprint, Carlisle, Pa.: Banner of Truth, 1982), 4:524.
67. John Owen, *Church Purity and Unity*, vol. 15 in *The Works of John Owen*, ed. William H. Goold (1850–53 edition; reprint, Carlisle, Pa.: Banner of Truth, 1965), 44.
68. For example, Archbishop John Whitgift wrote, "The Book of Common Prayer, and of ordering bishops, priests, and deacons, containeth nothing in it contrary to the Word of God." See "Archbishop Whitgift's Articles, 1583," in *The Tudor Constitution*, ed. G. R. Elton (Cambridge: Cambridge University Press, 1960), 444.
69. Preface to the 1549 prayer book, in *Two Liturgies*, ed. Ketley, 18.
70. Philip E. Hughes, *Theology of the English Reformers*, rev. ed. (Grand Rapids: Baker, 1980), 143. The entire discussion of Anglican worship is most helpful (pp. 141–58).
71. George Gillespie, *A Dispute against the English Popish Ceremonies*, in vol. 1 of *The Presbyterian's Armoury*, 3 vols. (1660; reprint, Edinburgh: Robert Ogle and Oliver and Boyd, 1846), 189.
72. Ibid.
73. Ibid., 191–92.
74. Ibid., 192.
75. Ibid., 193.
76. Davies, *Worship of the English Puritans*, 50.
77. Jordan, *Sociology of the Church*, 28.

CHAPTER 6: THY WILL BE DONE

1. Many of the prooftexts cited by proponents of the Puritan regulative principle of worship are exegeted well in the standard sources. Application, however, may be another matter. I have no argument with the exegesis and application of the biblical texts that address elements of worship. Likewise, there is no dispute over those texts that prescribe certain circumstances as necessary for the proper conduct of an element of worship. My contention is that some prooftexts are extended improperly to apply to matters that lie

beyond the scope of the text, matters that are truly circumstantial and in-different. For example, Leviticus 10:1–3 addresses the sin of Nadab and Abihu. Their offering of "strange fire" violated prescribed circumstances, and they were judged for disobeying the divine command. The relation of this text to circumstances that are neither forbidden nor commanded, *adiaphora*, is much more tenuous and, in my judgment, not compelling.

2. Edward Hindson, ed., *Introduction to Puritan Theology* (Grand Rapids: Guardian, 1976), 23. Likewise, John Leith, *Assembly at Westminster* (Atlanta: John Knox, 1973), 78–79.

3. Gregory Dix, *The Shape of the Liturgy* (London: A. C. Black, 1945; reprint, New York: Seabury, 1982), 312; also, James F. White, "Where the Reformation Was Wrong on Worship," *Christian Century*, 27 October 1962, 1076; James B. Jordan, *Sociology of the Church* (Tyler, Tex.: Geneva Ministries, 1986), 171; Robert Webber, *Worship Old and New* (Grand Rapids: Zondervan, 1982), 12–13.

4. Cornelius Van Til, *An Introduction to Systematic Theology*, vol. 5 in *In Defense of the Faith* (Phillipsburg, N.J.: Presbyterian and Reformed, 1978), 31–32.

5. Ibid., 35–36. See also Benjamin B. Warfield, "Authority, Intellect, Heart," in *Selected Shorter Writings of Benjamin B. Warfield*, 2 vols., ed. John H. Meeter (Nutley, N.J.: Presbyterian and Reformed, 1973), 2:668–71 for similar insights on this issue.

6. Joseph Crouch, *Puritanism and Art* (London: Cassell, 1910), 9.

7. John F. H. New, *Anglican and Puritan* (Stanford: Stanford University Press, 1969), 27–29.

8. See, for example, Gordon Rupp, "A Devotion of Rapture in English Puritanism," in *Reformation Conformity and Dissent*, ed. R. Buick Knox (London: Epworth, 1977), 115–31.

9. Geoffrey F. Nuttall, *The Puritan Spirit* (London: Epworth, 1967), 12; also, Leslie Rawlinson, "Worship in Liturgy and Form," in *Anglican and Puritan Thinking* (London: Westminster Conference, 1977), 85.

10. George Gillespie, *A Dispute against the English Popish Ceremonies*, in vol. 1 of *The Presbyterian's Armoury*, 3 vols. (1660; reprint, Edinburgh: Robert Ogle and Oliver and Boyd, 1846), 36.

11. Ibid., 37.

12. John Flavel, "Antipharmacum Saluberrimum," in *The Works of John Flavel*, 6 vols. (1820; reprint, Carlisle, Pa.: Banner of Truth, 1982), 4:525.

13. John Owen, *Church Unity and Purity*, vol. 15 in *The Works of John Owen*, ed. William H. Goold (1850–53 edition; reprint, Carlisle, Pa.: Banner of Truth, 1965), 467–68.

14. Rousas J. Rushdoony, *The Flight from Humanity* (Nutley, N.J.: Craig, 1973), 10.

15. Jordan, *Sociology of the Church*, 211.
16. Norman Fiering, *Moral Philosophy at Seventeenth-Century Harvard* (Chapel Hill: University of North Carolina Press, 1981), 152–54.
17. James Deotis Roberts Sr., *From Puritanism to Platonism in Seventeenth Century England* (The Hague: Martinus Nijhoff, 1968), 224; also, M. M. Knappen, *Tudor Puritanism* (Chicago: University of Chicago Press, 1939), 341.
18. J. I. Packer, "The Puritan Approach to Worship," in *Diversity in Unity*, papers read at the Puritan and Reformed Studies Conference, London, Dec. 1963, p. 5. Horton Davies, *The Worship of the English Puritans* (Westminster: Dacre, 1948), 258, gives similar examples that he describes as "bibliolatry."
19. Jordan, *Sociology of the Church*, 209.
20. This is Leith's warning concerning prooftexts; see *Assembly at Westminster*, 80.
21. As in George Gillespie, *A Treatise of Miscellany Questions*, in vol. 2 of *The Presbyterian's Armoury*, 3 vols. (1649; reprint, Edinburgh: Robert Ogle and Oliver and Boyd, 1846), 100–3.
22. For example, does Acts 1:26 really have any exegetical bearing on the question of the power of the ruling elder? See George Gillespie, *Assertion of the Government of the Church of Scotland*, in vol. 1 of *The Presbyterian's Armoury* (1641; reprint, Edinburgh: Robert Ogle and Oliver and Boyd, 1846), 35.
23. Gillespie, *Dispute against the English Popish Ceremonies*, 119–20.
24. John Murray, "Systematic Theology," *Westminster Theological Journal* 26.1 (Nov. 1963): 33.
25. Leith, *Assembly at Westminster*, 78–83.
26. Mark E. VanderSchaaf, "Archbishop Parker's Efforts toward a Bucerian Discipline in the Church of England," *Sixteenth Century Journal* 3.1 (April 1977): 101, refers to the Puritans' fascination with a "New Testament" church. Also, Jordan, *Sociology of the Church*, 209.
27. Owen, *Church Unity and Purity*, 14.
28. Ibid., 44; also, 462–65.
29. Rawlinson, "Worship," 85, notes the Puritans "believed that only what our Lord had commanded and what was commended by example in the New Testament were permissible."
30. Excepting, of course, ceremonial elements that have been fulfilled by the life or ministry of Christ and therefore are no longer binding in their Old Covenant form.
31. Exclusive psalmody and the ban on the instrumental accompaniment of singing (in public worship) are two separate issues, but frequently linked by proponents of the Puritan regulative principle of worship. The proponents of the Puritan regulative principle of worship are correct in maintaining that these are the historic views of Presbyterians. John L. Girardeau, *Instru-*

mental Music in Public Worship (1888; reprint, Havertown, Pa.: New Covenant Publication Society, 1983), provides the classic argument against the use of instumental music. Michael Bushell, *The Songs of Zion* (Pittsburgh: Crown and Covenant, 1977), provides a comprehensive argument for exclusive psalmody. The question is not, however, whether these views are historically correct. Instead, the question is whether they are biblically correct. For a helpful discussion of these issues, and some compelling arguments against these positions, see John M. Frame, *Worship in Spirit and Truth* (Phillipsburg, N.J.: Presbyterian and Reformed, 1996), 123–30.

32. John Murray, "The Worship of God in the Four Gospels," in *The Biblical Doctrine of Worship* (n.p.: Committee on Worship: Reformed Presbyterian Church of North America, 1974), 93.

33. Ibid., 95.

34. C. K. Barrett, *The Gospel according to St. John* (London: S.P.C.K., 1965), 199–200.

35. John Murray, "Worship of God in the Four Gospels," 96; emphasis added.

36. Abraham Millgram, *Jewish Worship* (Philadelphia: Jewish Publication Society of America, 1972), 64; note also Hayim Halevy Donin, *To Be a Jew* (New York: Basic Blocks, Inc., 1972), 183, where he refers to the synagogue's "very inception after the destruction of the First Temple in 586 B.C.E."

37. James B. Jordan, "Introduction," in *The Reconstruction of the Church*, vol. 4 in *Christianity and Civilization*, ed. James B. Jordan (Tyler, Tex.: Geneva Ministries, 1985), ix–x; idem, *Sociology of the Church*, 61. This is the argument of Joseph A. Pipa Jr., "Covenantal Worship," in *Written for Our Instruction*, ed. Joseph A. Pipa Jr. and J. Andrew Wortman (Taylors, S.C.: Southern Presbyterian, 2001), 78. For the origin of the synagogue, see the evidence summarized in *TDNT*, s.v. "*Sunagōgē.*" Some have tried to argue from Acts 15:21 that the synagogue goes back to the time of Moses. However, see Simon J. Kistemaker, *Acts*, New Testament Commentary (Grand Rapids: Baker, 1990), ad. loc. for a better understanding of the text.

38. Jordan, *Sociology of the Church*, 62.

39. Rousas J. Rushdoony, *The Institutes of Biblical Law* (n.p.: Presbyterian and Reformed, 1973), 130.

40. *ISBE*, s.v. "Synagogue," and ZPEB, s.v. "Synagogue."

41. Douglas Bannerman, *The Scripture Doctrine of the Church* (1887; reprint, Grand Rapids: Eerdmans, 1955), 155–56. Bannerman also argues for an exilic origin of the synagogue (p. 124).

42. One of Richard Hooker's objections to the Puritan position over four hundred years ago. See Richard Hooker, *Of the Laws of Ecclesiastical Polity, Books I–IV*, vol. 1 of the Folger Library edition of the Works of Richard Hooker, ed. W. Speed Hill (1593; reprint, Cambridge, Mass.: Belknap, 1977), 1:217.

43. Gillespie, *Dispute against the English Popish Ceremonies*, 116.

44. See the discussions in *ISBE*, s.v. "Worship," and *ZPEB*, s.v. "Worship."
45. Gillespie, *Dispute against the English Popish Ceremonies*, 116.
46. Millgram, *Jewish Worship*, 76. T. W. Manson, "The Jewish Background," in *Christian Worship*, ed. Nathaniel Micklem (London: Oxford University Press, 1936), 36–38, notes the significant influences that temple worship exerted on synagogue worship.
47. James H. Charlesworth, "A Prolegomenon to a New Study of the Jewish Background of the Hymns and Prayers in the New Testament," *Journal of Jewish Studies* 33.1–2 (spring-autumn 1982): 265.
48. A portion of the prophets closely linked with the Torah lection.
49. Scott Francis Brenner, *The Way of Worship* (New York: Macmillan, 1944), 6–8. Millgram, *Jewish Worship*, 89–120, expands these elements at length and gives examples of the benedictions and other liturgical elements in first-century worship.
50. Charlesworth, "Prolegomenon," 267.
51. Joseph A. Fitzmyer, *The Gospel according to Luke I–IX*, Anchor Bible vol. 28, ed. William F. Albright and David N. Freedman (Garden City, N.Y.: Doubleday, 1981), 530.
52. Alfred B. Edersheim labors this point at length in *The Life and Times of Jesus the Messiah*, one-volume edition (reprint, Grand Rapids: Eerdmans, 1981), part 1, pp. 451–53. Likewise, Fitzmyer, *Luke I–IX*, 530; Manson, "Jewish Background," 39, speaks of Jesus' "sharing in the most characteristic of the Synagogue activities."
53. Gary Cohen, *Biblical Separation Defended* (Philadelphia: Presbyterian and Reformed, 1966), 27.
54. Gustave Friedrich Oehler, *Theology of the Old Testament*, ed. George E. Day (Grand Rapids: Zondervan, n.d.), 323.
55. John's Gospel gives the most extensive coverage to Jesus' participation in the Jewish festivals (2:13; 6:4; 7:2). See Samuel J. Andrews, *The Life of Our Lord upon the Earth* (1906; reprint, Minneapolis: James family, 1978), 191.
56. Edersheim, *Life and Times of Jesus the Messiah*, part 2, pp. 226–27. Further historical data concerning the origin of this feast may be found in John Bright, *A History of Israel*, 3d ed. (Philadelphia: Westminster, 1981), 425–27. For a Jewish perspective, see Millgram, *Jewish Worship*, 268–70.
57. Interestingly enough, John Lightfoot urged Jesus' presence there to preach as justification for having a sermon during an assembly controversy over the observance of Christmas. See *The Journal of the Proceedings of the Assembly of Divines*, vol. 13 in *The Whole Works of the Rev. John Lightfoot, D.D.* (London: J. F. Dove, 1824), 191.
58. Edersheim, *Life and Times of Jesus the Messiah*, part 2, pp. 226–27.
59. Andrews, *Life of Our Lord upon the Earth*, 398.
60. Gillespie, *Dispute against the English Popish Ceremonies*, 124. He argues

against Purim as well. His arguments include: (1) Purim was civil only, and not religious (pp. 121–22); (2) if it were religious, Mordecai would be a prophet, so there would be a special warrant for the observation of Purim (p. 123); (3) it was unlawfully instituted, period (pp. 123–24). As may be noted, these objections include arguments based on silence, historical inaccuracies, and simple begging of the question. Similar arguments from "implication" or "good and necessary consequence" were expressed during the Westminster Assembly, session 649. The resolution states that "the fathers at first had a command from God . . . yet nothing is left recorded to show His will and appointment of the things instanced in, but the example and the practice of the apostles and the churches in their time." Mitchell, *Minutes of the Sessions of the Westminster Assembly of Divines*, 238. See also the essay by Jack Delivuk http://capo.org/premise/95/oct/p950907.html entitled, "Some Hermeneutical Methods in the Westminster Standards."

61. John Calvin, *Commentary on the Gospel according to John,* trans. William Pringle (1847; reprint, Grand Rapids: Baker, 1981), 412.

62. Leon Morris, *The Gospel according to John*, NICNT, ed. F. F. Bruce (Grand Rapids: Eerdmans, 1971), 299.

63. Raymond E. Brown, *The Gospel according to John (I–XII)*, Anchor Bible vol. 29, ed. William F. Albright and David N. Freedman (Garden City, N.Y.: Doubleday, 1966), 404–5.

64. John Murray, *Principles of Conduct* (Grand Rapids: Eerdmans, 1957), 150.

65. Morris, *John*, 516–17.

66. B. F. Westcott, *The Gospel according to St. John* (reprint, Grand Rapids: Eerdmans, 1975), 157. Also see p. 162 for arguments regarding the variant readings in the text.

67. Barrett, *John*, 320, comment on v. 36; Brown, *John (I–XII)*, 479.

68. Morris, *John*, 299.

69. See Bruce M. Metzger, *A Textual Commentary on the Greek New Testament* (New York: United Bible Societies, 1975), which gives the anarthrous reading (no definite article) an "A" rating, or virtual certainty.

CHAPTER 7: YOUR REASONABLE SERVICE

1. Paul Waitman Hoon, *The Integrity of Worship* (Nashville: Abingdon, 1971), 17.

2. Robert A. Morey, *Worship Is All of Life* (Camp Hill, Pa.: Christian Publications, 1984), 14–15.

3. Ibid., 22.

4. John MacArthur Jr., *The Ultimate Priority* (Chicago: Moody, 1983), viii.

5. Shepherd was formerly a professor of systematic theology at Westminster Theological Seminary and now is a retired minister in the Christian Reformed Church.

6. Norman Shepherd, "The Biblical Basis for the Regulative Principle of Worship," in *The Biblical Doctrine of Worship* (n.p.: Committee on Worship: Reformed Presbyterian Church of North America, 1974), 44–45.
7. Ibid., 44.
8. Ibid.
9. As seen below, the regulation of life does not involve *specific* commands *in extenso*; thus it would be hard to argue, by analogy, that worship must be subject to such extensive specification.
10. Michael Bushell, *The Songs of Zion* (Pittsburgh: Crown and Covenant, 1977), 26.
11. Cornelius Van Til, *Christian Theistic Ethics*, vol. 3 in *In Defense of the Faith* (Phillipsburg, N.J.: Presbyterian and Reformed, 1980), 34; also see *Common Grace and the Gospel* (Nutley, N.J.: Presbyterian and Reformed, 1977), 67.
12. Shepherd, "Biblical Basis," 45. Significantly, the "more pointed" reference to worship in the Carruthers text broadens the area of Christian liberty in matters of worship. S. W. Carruthers, ed., *The Westminster Confession of Faith* (Manchester: R. Aikman and Son, n.d.), 128.
13. Shepherd, "Biblical Basis," 44.
14. Bushell, *Songs*, 27.
15. John H. White, "Worship in the Pentateuch," in *The Biblical Doctrine of Worship* (n.p.: Committee on Worship: Reformed Presbyterian Church of North America, 1974), 11.
16. These are discussed in Ferdinand Hahn, *The Worship of the Early Church*, trans. David E. Green (Philadelphia: Fortress, 1973), 35–39; and C. F. D. Moule, *Worship in the New Testament* (London: Lutterworth, 1961), 67–81, esp. 79–81.
17. Hahn, *Worship of the Early Church*, 37. Although K. Hess explains certain references quite differently from Hahn, he generally agrees with Hahn's summary; see *NIDNTT*, s.v. "Serve, Deacon, Worship."
18. Moule, *Worship in the New Testament*, 80.
19. Used twenty-six times in the New Testament. See W. F. Moulton and A. S. Geden, *A Concordance to the Greek New Testament*, 5th rev. ed. (Edinburgh: T. and T. Clark, 1978), 584. See also Xavier Léon-Dufour, *Dictionary of the New Testament*, trans. Terrence Prendergast (San Francisco: Harper and Row, 1980), s.v. "Worship."
20. *NIDNTT*, s.v. "Serve, Deacon, Worship."
21. *TDNT*, s.v. "*latreuō, latreia*."
22. C. E. B. Cranfield, *The Epistle to the Romans*, 2 vols., ICC, ed. J. A. Emerton and C. E. B. Cranfield (Edinburgh: T. and T. Clark, 1979), 2:601.
23. H. Strathmann, in *TDNT*, s.v. "*leitourgeō, leitourgia, leitourgos, leitourgikos*."

24. *Dictionary of the New Testament*, s.v. "Worship."

25. Herman Ridderbos, *Paul: An Outline of His Theology*, trans. John Richard De Witt (Grand Rapids: Eerdmans, 1975), 481.

26. John M. Frame, *Worship in Spirit and Truth* (Phillipsburg, N.J.: Presbyterian and Reformed, 1996), 29.

27. Ibid., 31–32.

28. ZPEB, s.v., "Law in the Old Testament."

29. Ibid.

30. John M. Frame, *The Doctrine of the Knowledge of God* (Phillipsburg, N.J.: Presbyterian and Reformed, 1987), 67–68.

31. See the discussion in Gary Friessen, *Decision Making and the Will of God* (Portland, Ore.: Multnomah, 1980), 181–99, "Competent to Choose."

32. Francis A. Schaeffer, *Whatever Happened to the Human Race?* in *The Complete Works of Francis A. Schaeffer*, 2d ed., 5 vols. (Westchester, Ill.: Crossway, 1982), 5:385–86.

33. William H. Willimon, *The Service of God* (Nashville: Abingdon, 1983), 15–19.

34. Van Til, *Christian Theistic Ethics*, 44. Here, Van Til articulates a structure that parallels, in some ways, the "indicative" and "imperative" dynamic in Pauline thought. Cf. the discussion in Ridderbos, *Paul: An Outline of His Theology*, 253–58.

35. Van Til, *Christian Theistic Ethics*, 45.

36. Ibid.

37. Ibid., 45–46.

38. Ibid., 45.

39. Ibid., 48.

40. Ibid., 49.

41. Ibid., 53.

42. Herman Dooyeweerd, *Roots of Western Culture*, trans. John Kraay (Toronto: Wedge, 1979), 73–81, argues that inherent in creation itself is the impetus for differentiation in culture. "Cultural differentiation is necessary so that the creational ordinance, which calls for the disclosure or unfolding of everything in accordance with its inner nature, may be realized also in historical development" (p. 74).

43. Van Til, *Christian Theistic Ethics*, 80.

44. Ibid., 81.

45. Herman N. Ridderbos, *The Epistle of Paul to the Churches of Galatia*, trans. Henry Zylstra, NICNT, ed. F. F. Bruce (Grand Rapids: Eerdmans, 1953), 15.

46. Johannes Munck, *The Acts of the Apostles*, Anchor Bible vol. 31, ed. William F. Albright and David N. Freedman (Garden City, N.Y.: Doubleday, 1981), 155.

47. F. F. Bruce, *Commentary on the Book of Acts*, NICNT, ed. F. F. Bruce (Grand Rapids: Eerdmans, 1977), 322.

48. Ibid. Bruce observes (n. 7) that even in regard to the situation in Galatia, Paul treated circumcision as an indifferent matter. He objected to it when it became a matter of religious obligation.

49. The evidence indicates that circumcision was still a family ceremony and had not yet entered into the synagogue liturgy. The question of circumcision, then, is not directly related to the nature of corporate worship. Nevertheless, the relevance to our discussion is the fact that circumcision, an "element" of Old Testament Jewish covenantal faithfulness, had now become merely circumstantial and indifferent.

50. Munck, *Acts*, 212.

51. Bruce, *Acts*, 432 n. 39.

52. John Murray, "The Weak and the Strong," in John Murray, *Collected Writings of John Murray*, 4 vols. (Carlisle, Pa.: Banner of Truth, 1976–82), 4:143.

53. Ibid.; also, Cranfield, *Romans*, 2:690.

54. Murray, "The Weak and the Strong," 145.

55. Cranfield, *Romans*, 2:696–97.

56. Murray, "The Weak and the Strong," 155.

57. Cranfield, *Romans*, 2:713, limits the application to the ceremonies of the law, but Murray, "The Weak and the Strong," 154–55, expands the passage to apply to anything God has created. Even if one grants Cranfield's limited exegetical import, by application (as well as other NT evidence, 1 Tim. 4:4–5) there is valid reason to apply the text to every part of creation not otherwise forbidden.

58. W. Sanday and A. C. Headlam, *The Epistle to the Romans*, 5th ed., ICC, ed. S. R. Driver, A. Plummer, and C. A. Briggs (1902; reprint, Edinburgh: T. and T. Clark, 1977), 402.

59. Murray, "The Weak and the Strong," 157.

60. "Something which had a religious character and influence"; Charles Hodge, *Commentary on the First Epistle to the Corinthians* (reprint, Grand Rapids: Eerdmans, 1972), 146.

61. Archibald Robertson and Alfred Plummer, *A Critical and Exegetical Commentary on the First Epistle of St. Paul to the Corinthians*, 2d ed., ICC, ed. S. R. Driver, A. Plummer, and C. A. Briggs (1911; reprint, Edinburgh: T. and T. Clark, 1975), 170.

62. Gordon D. Fee, *The First Epistle to the Corinthians*, NICNT, ed. F. F. Bruce (Grand Rapids: Eerdmans, 1987), 384.

63. Robertson and Plummer, *First Epistle of St. Paul to the Corinthians*, 170.

64. Augsburg Confession, article 7, "De potestate ecclesiastica," in Philip Schaff, *The Creeds of Christendom*, 6th ed., 3 vols., revised by David Schaff (1931; reprint, Grand Rapids: Baker, 1983), 3:58ff.

65. Formula of Concord, in Schaff, *Creeds*, 3:160–61.

66. Ibid., ad. loc.
67. Ibid., 162.
68. Belgic Confession, in Schaff, *Creeds*, 3:423–24.
69. P. Y. De Jong, *The Church's Witness to the World* (St. Catharines, Ont.: Paideia, 1980), 2:323.
70. Scotch Confession of Faith (1560), in Schaff, *Creeds*, 3:465.
71. Second Helvetic Confession, in Schaff, *Creeds*, 3:875, 277.
72. Thirty-Nine Articles, in Schaff, *Creeds*, 3:500.
73. Ibid., 3:508–9 (article 33).
74. Carruthers, ed. *Westminster Confession of Faith*, 127.

CHAPTER 8: IN LIGHT OF THE COVENANT

1. J. J. von Allmen, *Worship: Its Theology and Practice* (New York: Oxford University Press, 1965), 96.
2. John M. Frame, *Worship in Spirit and Truth* (Phillipsburg, N.J.: Presbyterian and Reformed, 1996), 38–43, seeks to substitute "applications" for "circumstances." By changing the terms, he seeks to resolve the same problem I address through the rehabilitation of *adiaphora* and the expansion of circumstances. I have chosen to use the categories "elements" and "circumstances" because they are conventional language for this discussion.
3. Von Allmen, *Worship: Its Theology and Practice*, 96.
4. Vern S. Poythress, *Symphonic Theology* (Grand Rapids: Zondervan, 1987), 52, notes that everyone labors with preconceptions and biases. This need not be destructive. As he says: "by using a bias self-consciously, we put ourselves in a better position to remember that our discoveries have arisen from *one* starting point among many."
5. Geerhardus Vos, "The Idea of Biblical Theology as a Science and as a Theological Discipline," in *Redemptive History and Biblical Interpretation*, ed. Richard B. Gaffin Jr. (Phillipsburg, N.J.: Presbyterian and Reformed, 1980), 11–14.
6. Geerhardus Vos, "Paul's Eschatological Concept of the Spirit," in *Redemptive History and Biblical Interpretation*, ed. Richard B. Gaffin Jr. (Phillipsburg, N.J.: Presbyterian and Reformed, 1980), 103.
7. See Rom. 8:4–9, 14; 1 Cor. 12:3, 13; 14:15–16.
8. Von Allmen, *Worship: Its Theology and Practice*, 102.
9. Ibid.
10. Francis A. Schaeffer, *Genesis in Space and Time*, in *The Complete Works of Francis Schaeffer*, 2d ed., 5 vols. (Westchester, Ill.: Crossway, 1982), 40.
11. Rousas J. Rushdoony, *The Institutes of Biblical Law* (n.p.: Presbyterian and Reformed, 1973), 9.

12. L. Kalsbeek, *Contours of a Christian Philosophy* (Toronto: Wedge, 1975), 74.
13. Augustine, for example, speaks of liberty from sin as being able to obey God's commands. See Augustine, "The Enchiridion," in *Basic Writings of Augustine*, ed. Whitney J. Oates, 2 vols. (1948; reprint, Grand Rapids: Baker, 1980), 1:675, chapter 30.
14. Robert A. Morey, *Worship Is All of Life* (Camp Hill, Pa.: Christian Publications, 1984), 82.
15. Poythress, *Symphonic Theology*, 53.
16. C. E. B. Cranfield, *The Epistle to the Romans*, 2 vols., ICC, ed. J. A. Emerton and C. E. B. Cranfield (Edinburgh: T. and T. Clark, 1979), 2:729, says "*pistis* here denotes one's confidence that one's faith (in the basic NT sense of the word) allows one to do a particular thing."
17. Howard G. Hageman, *Pulpit and Table* (Richmond: John Knox, 1962), 109.
18. Paul Anderson, "Balancing Form and Freedom," *Leadership* 7.2 (spring 1986): 24–33, argues for the necessity of balancing form and freedom within every service of worship. He also provides suggestions for implementing such a practice. See also Robert Webber, *Worship Is a Verb* (Waco: Word, 1985), 133–34.
19. James B. Jordan, *The Sociology of the Church* (Tyler, Tex.: Geneva Ministries, 1986), 25.
20. Webber, *Worship Is a Verb*, 110.
21. Robert G. Rayburn, *O Come, Let Us Worship* (Grand Rapids: Baker, 1980), 16–17.
22. Ralph P. Martin, *The Worship of God* (Grand Rapids: Eerdmans, 1982), 217–28, has an excellent discussion of this dialogic movement in worship. See also Rayburn, *O Come, Let Us Worship*, 118–29, "Worship as Dialogue."
23. Warren W. Wiersbe, *Real Worship* (Nashville: Oliver Nelson, 1986), 108.
24. Jordan, *Sociology of the Church*, 25.
25. Ronald Allen and Gordon Borror, *Worship: Rediscovering the Missing Jewel* (Portland, Ore.: Multnomah, 1982), 57.
26. Cf. 1 Cor. 1:2 and 11:16.
27. Gordon D. Fee, *The First Epistle to the Corinthians*, NICNT, ed. F. F. Bruce (Grand Rapids: Eerdmans, 1987), 698. He surveys possible interpretations of verse 33 on pages 696–98.
28. Charles Hodge, *Commentary on the First Epistle to the Corinthians* (reprint, Grand Rapids: Eerdmans, 1972), 305.
29. Richard B. Gaffin Jr., "On Being Reformed," *Bulletin of Westminster Theological Seminary* 24.4 (fall 1985).
30. Ibid.
31. Poythress, *Symphonic Theology*, 52.
32. Von Allmen, *Worship: Its Theology and Practice*, 49.

33. Geoffrey Wainwright, "The Understanding of Liturgy in the Light of Its History," in *The Study of Liturgy*, ed. Cheslyn Jones, Geoffrey Wainwright, and Edward Yarnold (New York: Oxford University Press, 1978), 495.

34. Charles Hodge, *Systematic Theology*, 3 vols. (reprint, Grand Rapids: Eerdmans, 1977), 1:115–16 and 1:123–27, discusses the closely related issue of "common consent" of the church, *consensus fidelium*. Hodge, although denying the Roman Catholic understanding of the term, admits there is some value in common consent, providing it is in accordance with Scripture, and not contrary to it.

35. Hageman, *Pulpit and Table*, 128.

36. Chuck Kraft, "World View and Worship," *Worship Times* 2.1 (spring 1987): 2.

37. Eugene and Helen Westra, "Let All the Earth Worship the Lord," *Reformed Worship* 3 (spring 1987): 9.

38. Nicholas P. Wolterstorff, "The Genius of Reformed Liturgy," *Reformed Worship* 2 (winter 1986/87): 10.

39. Robert Webber, "Worship East and West," *Worship Times* 2.1 (spring 1987): 3.

40. James H. Olthuis, "Worship and Witness," in *Will All the King's Men*, ed. James H. Olthuis et al. (Toronto: Wedge, 1972), 21.

41. Anscar J. Chupungco, *Cultural Adaptation of the Liturgy* (New York: Paulist, 1982), 20.

42. Olthuis, "Worship and Witness," 23.

43. Appianda Arthur, "The African Missionary's Legacy: Sharing the Gospel, Taking Away the Culture," *Worship Times* 2.1 (spring 1987): 7.

44. Joseph Gelineau, "Tradition-Invention-Culture," in *Liturgy: A Creative Tradition*, ed. Mary Collins and David Power, Concilium (New York: Seabury, 1983), 11.

45. Jordan, *Sociology of the Church*, 222.

46. Mark Brasler, "Sensitive to the Senses," *Leadership* 7.2 (spring 1986): 21.

47. Webber, *Worship Is a Verb*, 21, encourages the church to pay more attention to right brain (aesthetic, versus left brain, analytic) activity in worship. Such worship would appeal to all senses (one of the great values in weekly communion) including touch, taste, sight, and smell (along with hearing, of course).

48. Sacred, not in opposition to profane, but as peculiarly devoted to the public act of worship.

49. Webber, *Worship Is a Verb*, 23.

50. But James F. White, "Our Apostasy in Worship," *Christian Century*, 28 September, 1977, 842, indicts Protestant churches for failing to give proper place to the Scriptures in corporate worship. His complaint still seems appropriate at the beginning of the twenty-first century.

51. Paul Waitman Hoon, *The Integrity of Worship* (Nashville: Abingdon, 1971), 314, says the lack of balance between body and soul in worship results in "the sickness of passivity in many Protestant congregations today."

52. Von Allmen, *Worship: Its Theology and Practice*, 154.
53. Acts 2:46; 20:7; 1 Cor. 11:20. See also Oscar Cullmann, *Early Christian Worship*, trans. A. Stewart Todd and James B. Torrance (Philadelphia: Westminster, 1953), 29; Josef A. Jungmann, *The Early Liturgy*, trans. Francis A. Brunner, vol. 6 in *Liturgical Studies* (Notre Dame: University of Notre Dame Press, 1959), 29–38.
54. Von Allmen, *Worship*, 64–66; Meredith Kline, *By Oath Consigned* (Grand Rapids: Eerdmans, 1967), 73–83.
55. Jordan, *Sociology of the Church*, 244–46.
56. Max Thurian, *The One Bread*, trans. Theodore DuBois (New York: Sheed and Ward, 1969), 19.
57. Robert Webber, *Worship Old and New* (Grand Rapids: Zondervan, 1982), 16–19.
58. Martin, *Worship of God*, 211.
59. Webber, *Worship Old and New*, 91.
60. Von Allmen, *Worship: Its Theology and Practice*, 37.
61. T. F. Torrance, *Theology in Reconciliation* (Grand Rapids: Eerdmans, 1975), 133–34. Of course, Torrance distances himself from the "representation" of Tridentine Roman Catholic theology, noting that "his Offering is once for all and does not need to be repeated" (p. 133).
62. Martin, *Worship of God*, 211.
63. Torrance, *Theology in Reconciliation*, 134.
64. Von Allmen, *Worship: Its Theology and Practice*, 34.
65. Torrance, *Theology in Reconciliation*, 110; von Allmen, *Worship: Its Theology and Practice*, 23–24.
66. Torrance, *Theology in Reconciliation*, 134.
67. Ibid., 110–11.
68. Vern S. Poythress, "Ezra 3, Union with Christ, and Exclusive Psalmody," *Westminster Theological Journal* 37 (May 1975): 221.
69. See Richard B. Gaffin Jr., *Perspectives on Pentecost* (Phillipsburg, N.J.: Presbyterian and Reformed, 1979), 118–22.

INDEX OF SUBJECTS
AND NAMES

INDEX OF CONFESSIONS
AND CATECHISMS

R. J. Gore Jr. is professor of systematic theology, as well as dean, at Erskine Theological Seminary. Before coming to Erskine, he served as pastor of a Presbyterian Church and has been a chaplain in the army reserves since 1986.

Gore holds four master's degrees, including the M.A. in dogmatic theology from St. Charles Borromeo Seminary. He received the Ph.D. in historical and theological studies from Westminster Theological Seminary.

He has contributed articles to several theological journals, including the *Journal of the Evangelical Theological Society, Presbyterion: Covenant Seminary Review,* and the *Westminster Theological Journal.*

He and his wife, Joan, have three children.